The Diary of a Confederate Soldier
JAMES E. HALL

*The Diary of
A Confederate Soldier*
JAMES E. HALL

Edited by
RUTH WOODS DAYTON

Copyright © 1961 by Elizabeth Teter Phillips
Copyright © 2020 by Commonwealth Book Company
All Rights Reserved
Printed in the United States of America
ISBN: 978-1-948986-20-5

THE PARENTAGE OF JAMES EDMOND HALL

The Hall family is of English-French descent, the first to emigrate to America arriving in 1745.

Samuel and Elizabeth Owens Hall were early settlers in that part of Virginia later to become the State of West Virginia. They lived for a time in Lewis County, where their son John N. (father of James E. Hall) was born, Sept. 30, 1815. The following year the family moved to Barbour County, purchasing a farm on Elk Creek, near Philippi, which became their permanent home.

The son John, following the pattern set by his father, became a farmer and stock raiser, as well as a public official. He served for twenty years as Justice of the Peace, and was later elected President of the Barbour County Court, a position he held for four years. In 1834 he married Harriet (born Jan. 29, 1815), daughter of John and Anna Rightmire, from the adjoining county of Harrison, where her father was a merchant. John and Harriet Hall were the parents of five children:

1. Julia (Julee) born 1835.

2. Almira J. (Allie) born 1837. Married Joseph N. B. Crim.

3. Emma born 1840. Married Col. N. J. Coplin.
4. JAMES EDMOND HALL born Nov. 27, 1841. Died Jan. 1, 1915.
5. Jasper L. born 1845. Attorney. Elected W. Va. State Senate 1872; House of Delegates 1881. Died in New Mexico.

After a boyhood spent on his father's farm, James E. Hall was sent to school in Morgantown at the Monongalia Academy—forerunner of the West Virginia University.

With the imminence of war, he returned to his home, where he joined a newly organized local Militia Company called The Barbour Greys. This Company was mustered into the Confederate Army as Company H 31st Virginia Infantry, on May 14, 1861, and on this date, with the lowly rank of Fourth Corporal, James E. Hall began his years of war service.

ACKNOWLEDGMENT

In this Diary my grandfather records that after his exchange as a prisoner of war, he received a forty-day furlough. Attempting to return to his home, he traveled chiefly on foot, until he reached Staunton. There, Samuel Woods of Philippi, a Confederate officer in charge of Quartermaster Supplies, loaned him a horse.

Mr. Woods, later a Judge of the Supreme Court of West Virginia, was the grandfather of my lifelong friend, Ruth Woods Dayton, who, at my request, undertook the tedious and time-consuming task of editing this almost illegible record of a century ago.

I wish not only to acknowledge my gratitude to her for helping to make its publication possible, but to also acknowledge my indebtedness for her grandfather's kindness to a fellow soldier.

                      Elizabeth Teter Phillips
                      Philippi, West Virginia

October 1961

FOREWORD

The truth of the famous statement made by a Civil War general that "War is Hell" has never been questioned nor denied.

Military records have given the cold, concise facts of victory and defeat; officers have filed reports and written tactical memoirs; strategists have published countless volumes explaining why the defeats occurred, and how the victories could have been more expertly contrived.

Yet it is possible that none of these are more convincing of war's dread meaning than the stark details revealed in this Diary of a twenty-year-old volunteer. In it are found not only the reasons why War is Hell, but also are found the evidences of a sustaining hope and faith that endured through four cruel years of exhaustion, hunger, exposure to freezing cold and drenching rain, and of neglected illness; through the strain and shock of battle, the suffering of a wound; through capture, and nineteen months spent in the bleak confinement of enemy prison camps.

Though a century has passed since James Edmond Hall made the first entry in his little six and a half by four inch Diary, and though its penciled pages are faded and worn, Time has not dimmed its poignant, human appeal, nor diminished the historic value of this personal document of the Civil War.

>Ruth Woods Dayton
>Lewisburg, West Virginia

October 1961

1861

Philippi, Va. May— 1861

I have volunteered in the Confederate Army. Having just returned from a distant school, and the bright anticipations of a brilliant future, I can not fully visualize the stern realities of war. Hardships, heretofore and even now unknown, will evidently follow every camp occupant, and scenes of carnage and death await a soldier's soliloquy. Be it so. We will go farther, and consider our lives as a small offering for our native land! May God avert the danger which now so innocently threatens her.

A few days with my much loved sisters, and the most indulgent of parents, and I leave again.

Early this morning our commander Capt. A. G. Reger, informed us to leave at 12 the same day. When we left we knew we were bound for Beverly, to meet at that place a train of ammunition, arms, etc. and guard them from thence to Philippi. Our reception in Beverly was very cordial. Bouquets were thrown before us by *fairy* hands, and aged citizens came to welcome us. Next morning a command of 700 men came from eastern counties and were bound for Grafton, Va. Our company joined the same command and started for Philippi. The walk was very fatiguing, inasmuch as I was wholly unused to it. We arrived at Philippi on the morning of May . . . , amid the most enthusiastic demonstrations of joy by assembled citizens. We remained there until the . . . of May. The principal part of the command having preceded us to Grafton. The first day we went to Fetterman, remained there a day, and then went to Grafton. We suffered considerably in the meantime from the walk and the want of food.

On the morning of . . . May, 1861 we were informed that the Federals were assembled about Grafton in considerable force. We hourly anticipated an attack, and for the first time experienced those feelings which are common to most young soldiers before an engagement. Our commander, Col. Porterfield however, determined to retreat. We marched to Philippi that day through various alarms of the enemy's pursuit. At Philippi we received a small reinforcement. I was well satisfied there—being in the society of many of my most intimate friends. I could not be with them much however. I then thought our commanders were unjust in having such rigid discipline—especially for Volunteers. I am used to it now.

We remained in Philippi until the 3rd of June. Early on that morning we were startled from beds by the firing of the enemy's cannon. The shells fell thick and fast among us, wounding a few. Col. Porterfield immediately ordered a retreat. We marched to Beverly the same day, a distance of 38 miles. We were much exhausted. When we arrived, my cousin Will Jarvis and I entered a deserted dwelling—most of the citizens on hearing the cannonading had left—and immediately laid ourselves down on the naked floor of the hall and soundly slept, our canteens serving us for pillows.

The next morning was dark and gloomy. The clouds were hanging around the summit of the distant mountains, and the rain fell in torrents. We remained the whole of that day—June 4—and at night started for Huttonsville. The fatigue of that march I shall never forget. The mud was very deep and the creeks much swollen by the recent rains. We, blindly almost, urged ourselves onward, and arrived at Huttonsville early next morning. I there met my aunt Mary Davidson, and my cousins Betty and Jane Armstrong. They gave me a cup of highly flavored coffee and plenty of light bread, a luxury which we have but rarely enjoyed since.

We remained there until the 15th of June. In the meantime I received a package from my sister, Al Crim, containing a blanket, oilcloth and various other articles,—we having lost all our baggage on our retreat. The evening we started from Huttonsville was very pleasant. The soldiers appeared very much pleased with the movement, and amid cheers, left at double quick step. We marched that night to the foot of Laurel Hill. We separated however, from a part of the command at Beverly, which went to defend the Rich Mountain Pass. They were under the command of Col. Heck, afterward superseded by Col. Pegram. We were under the immediate command of Gen. R. S. Garnett. Next morning we advanced to the western side of the mountain and encamped.

Then commenced a series of hardships pertaining to camp life, especially where but few comforts can be had for soldiers. The cooking department was the greatest obstacle. Our mess consisted of Dr. Armstrong, W. D. F. Jarvis, M. M. Rider, Lieuts. G. T. Thompson and I. V. Johnson, my brother Jasper and myself; and none knew the first principles of cooking. We learned however, very rapidly. We stayed there, —going through regular drills every day until the . . . of July. On the . . . Sunday the Yankees advanced upon us from Philippi. General Garnett sent the First Georgia Regt. out to check their advance.—The roar of their guns we could but indistinctly hear as we were on picket guard on the top of the mountain. We were relieved the following evening.

On the evening of . . . July our company was detached for guard. We accompanied Col. Taliaferro's Regt. which went to relieve the skirmishers. We stopped a few hundred yards from the enemy's outpost. The Regt. went on and engaged the enemy. We were sheltered from the balls by a huge log. We remained on our post until morning, when the enemy's fire became so hot, we retired nearer our camp, but not out of range of their guns. They endeavored to drive the whole guard back to camp, and to accomplish it, shot cannon balls, case shot and canister at us for near ten hours. We were sheltered from them however, by the large trees of the woods. Several of us came very near being struck by their balls nevertheless. A few having the mud and dirt thrown over them by the explosion of shells. We picked up a few of their balls. A six pounder was sent down the road and fired some six shots at a house which was occupied by the Yankees. The house was utterly demolished. The enemy ceased firing when they heard the discharge of our gun. We were shortly relieved, and on the following evening went with our Regt. out as skirmishers. We engaged the enemy and had a brisk fire for a few minutes.

Next morning we began cooking provisions for 4 days. We were not yet done when the command "fall in" was heard all around. We immediately formed lines and commenced our line of march,—a retreat. Our intention was to go by way of Beverly, but finding the road blockaded, the entire command changed directions to go through the counties of Preston, Tucker, Hardy, etc. We there understood that the entire command of Cols. Heck and Pegram was either killed or taken prisoner. We marched all that day, and at night encamped on the opposite bank of Shavers Fork of Cheat River, without anything to eat and much fatigued by the march.

Next morning we started early, crossing this same stream as many as three times in as many miles. About noon that day we first became aware of the presence of the enemy. They overtook our rear guard at Cheat River. A terrible fire ensued. Our artillery firing into their ranks of four deep, at the distance of 200 yards. The cries of the wounded could be heard, and the flying of their guns into the air when struck by our shells, could be distinctly seen by our men. Nobly did our men repel the advancing foe. Cheat River ran red with their blood as they attempted to charge our columns. After 2 hours of hard fighting, our forces retired from so unequal a contest, but not until our brave commander Gen. Garnett, had fallen. (Carricks Ford, July 13.) The enemy then ceased their pursuit. They having lost about 700 men and we only 16.

It is said authentically that the Northern Commander Gen. McClellan shed tears of sympathy over the body of our brave but fallen hero. They having fought together, side by side on the plains of Buena Vista, were reared together, and were warm personal friends until the present war. Truly from the dawn of man's existence he is a creature of change. Mutation is surely a cardinal principle of his being.

After advancing a few miles further we were informed that our retreat would soon be intercepted by forces from West Union. Two pieces of artillery were brought up to the advance. We had no engagement however. It was over two days since we had eaten anything, and had been marching continually through the rain and mud, often crossing streams when three or four would have to lock hand to maintain their equilibrium. We now passed several wagons of ammunition and ordnance, the teams being unable to carry them farther. We also trampled over the finest clothing, linens, stacks of knapsacks and haversacks lying in heaps, together with everything necessary for a well fitted army. That night, I with some others, could proceed no further. We laid down by the side of the road with no protection, but not withstanding we slept soundly, not knowing it had rained upon us till morning when we awoke.

Next morning we started eastward over the mountains, and after five days of the most fatiguing walking, and narrow escape of the enemy, we arrived in Romney, Hampshire County. Meeting with some acquaintances, we remained two days, before starting for our army, then stationed at Monterey, Highland Co., a distance of 90 miles. We arrived there on the ... day of ... and met many kind friends who were driven from Philippi. The day after our arrival we received a pass to join our Regt. then stationed at Laurel, some 12 miles west of Monterey on the summit of the Allegheny Mountain. We then met with a portion of our company. Many having been left on the retreat. We remained there until the . . . , when we moved our camp four miles westward. At our new encampment we remained until the ... of . . . , when the whole number of Regiments belonging to this Division of the Army marched to a branch of the Greenbrier River, which is about 10 miles from the Cheat Mountain Pass—where there are Yankees, rattlesnakes and bears. *A onme id genus.* (Note: All of a kind.)

A few days after our arrival, a detachment of near 2000 men started to the mountains for the purpose of attacking the Federal Army. We were, however, misled by our guide and the enterprise consequently failed. It rained on us almost continually while in the mountains. Our provisions became perfectly saturated, and we were wet for two days in those chilly rains, without provisions.

Nothing of importance has transpired up to the time in which I write today.

NOTICE!!!
Sept. 7 . . .
> If I should be so unfortunate as to be slain in any battle, and if any (black-hearted) kind Yankee should find this on my carcass while looking for other things of far greater value, of which I have not any amount, I will be much obliged to him to send it to Miss Emma I. Hall, Elk Creek, Barbour Co. Va. I will be much obliged to any persons to do likewise, if they should find it after I lose it.
> James E. Hall
> Camp Bartow, Sept. 7, '61

Today, Sept. 9, a detachment of a few Regts. prepared provisions for four days, with the intention of going—we all presume—to attack the enemy on Cheat Mountain. Somebody will evidently "be hurt", as we are almost hourly expecting a decided movement at Lee's command, which is about 30 miles south of us, and only about 3 miles from the main body of the Federal Army.

Sept. 10 . . . We have no news from our men

who left us yesterday. They are however on Cheat Mountain a few miles south of the Pass. Our artillery, comprising about 8 guns, with one rifle piece, have orders to march this evening with the remainder of Col. Johnson's command. We do not know where they are going, but we can form I think, very correct opinions.

Today I visited the burial ground of our army. Feelings of gloomy sadness presented themselves while viewing the long line of graves—a little hillock of dirt forming their only monument. I meditate upon the desolation of a death in such a place and under such circumstances, and also of the grief of kind and loved friends far away in the sunny south. I entered the house—a deserted dwelling—which was filled with the sick. Many were rapidly failing. I saw many there who appeared so intellectual and highly educated, who undoubtedly were bright ornaments to the society in which they moved, leaving the world in such a place. I involuntarily breathed a prayer to their Creator who knows all, to be propitiator to their souls.

Sept. 12, 1861. The detachment that left here yesterday with our artillery, went as we supposed to the mountains. We were momentarily expecting to hear the roar of guns. We have already heard a few shots, probably from some picket post of the enemy. What should we do if we should sustain a defeat! I have no fears however, for our success.

Sept. 13. Friday. The detachment under Col. Rust returned this evening. Their provisions were exhausted. They brought in several prisoners, and had obtained the road in the rear of the enemy—cutting off all communication. Heavy firing was heard from Gen. Lee's command.

Sept. 14 . . . The expedition under Col. Rust that returned last night, stated that the Pass on the mountain that is occupied by the Yankees, is almost impregnable. They were prepared for our flanking party—having barricaded their entire encampment. Our men captured 3 wagons, 6 horses, 7 prisoners, together with one poor devil they killed. The men were entirely exhausted. The road can not be described, but is known to all mountaineers. This command is ordered out tomorrow morning, having provisions for four days. We have no idea where they are destined to operate.

Sept. 15 . . . Nothing of interest occurred today. A detachment of a few thousand men left this evening,—for, we suppose—Lee's command. They took their tents and provisions for 5 days.

Sept. 16 . . . The command which left here yesterday, returned today. They marched about 12 miles in the direction of Gen. Lee's command, and on receiving orders there from him, came back. The mud was excessively deep, and troops are much dejected and discouraged. This is a great place for the blues, at least with myself.

Sept. 17 . . . Nothing of importance has transpired. The Lee party left here for Petersburg this evening, and a few Regts. are going to start for the same place tomorrow. I have been on picket guard all day. The post is in a dense pine wood, so much so that the rays of the sun can hardly penetrate through the heavy foliage. I have been more discouraged today than I have since I have been in the army. I have given up the hope of getting home this winter. I also, had good health and a good constitution before joining the army, but now I begin to feel the effects of so much exposure. . . . I have the blues terribly . . . undoubtedly there is enough reason for me to feel melancholy. All my friends are at home—among the Yankees (Note: Philippi had been occupied by Federal troops since the battle there, June 3) excepting my brother, sixteen years old, who left the army some time ago, and who is staying among an aristocratic people, and is a stranger to them all. Shall we ever meet again in the quiet halls of home?

Sept. 18 . . . No men arriving today.

Sept. 19 . . . We are now going through the

same regular routine of drills and camp labor as heretofore. A few days before the expedition against the enemy, everything of the sort was stopped,—evidently eclipsed by the magnitude of the enterprise. Its proving a failure has had a very discouraging effect upon the troops. We, however have lost nothing, as we maintain our former position. True, we lost about 50 men by sickness, occasioned by the extreme exposure. — An instance of their exposure on the mountain— One young man became so chilled as to be rendered wholly insensible, and was with much difficulty revived.

Sept. 20 . . . No news today. Excepting that I heard from my brother Jasper in rather an unpleasant way— by the presenting of a *due bill* of $15.00.

Sept. 21 . . . We are yet going through the same regular routine of drills that we have heretofore.

Sept. 22 . . . Nothing of importance has occurred today. I heard from home indirectly, Mr. Jim Hanger brought a letter for me from Emma to Staunton, and sent it from there to Monterey. I have not received it yet, but am anxiously expecting it. John H. Hite brought me some elegant peaches, grapes and apples from Staunton.

Monday, Sept. 23 . . . Affairs still remain as cool as a cucumber . . . we are however, acting on the defensive. Throwing up breast works.

Tuesday, Sept. 24 . . . Today we heard that Gens. Floyd and Wise obtained a great and signal victory over the Federal forces in the south west. (W. Va.) It is only a rumor. We are busily engaged in throwing up entrenchments, and evidently are acting on the defensive. It is possible that we may be attacked, but we think it hardly probable.

Wednesday, Sept. 25 . . . Nothing new has transpired today. I am anxiously expecting a letter from home.

Thursday, Sept. 26 . . . I have the blues terribly. A little hope arrived a few days since, caused by the movement of Gen. Lee's army. I would, above all considerations like to winter in Western Virginia. It appears to me, that all a man would wish for, or for which he could desire, are concentrated in the pleasure of a quiet home. Surely, if during the revolutions of human affairs we may successfully unite ourselves in the old halls of home, I will never leave again. Could I ever again desire the exciting scenes of war? I have had enough now. I heard today that the enemy had shamefully treated some of the citizens of my County, respecting private property and personal violence. May the God of truth and justice forever curse them with His rod, for such infernal enactments.

The cooking department is again beginning to be a subject of much controversy. We are all getting tired of biscuit, beef and coffee without any change.

Butter demands	.25 cents per lb.
Cheese	" "
Eggs	" " per doz.
Chickens (cooked)	.50 cents
Turkeys (small)	$2.00
Corn Bread	.10 cents per lb.
Apple Butter	.20 cents per pt.
Potatoes	$1.50 per bu.

All the above are very scarce at those rates, but everyone purchases at any price. Sometimes we give them a cursing and march them out of camp at double quick—and then half starve for the fun!

Friday, Sept. 27

Good news from home, good news for me
Has come across the deep blue sea
From friends that I've not seen for years,
From friends that I have left in tears.

No father near to guide me now
No mother's tears to soothe my brow
No sister's voice falls on my ear
Nor brother's smile to give me cheer.

And since we parted long ago
My life has been a scene of woe
But now a joyful hour is come
For I have had good news from home.

Although I have wandered far away
My heart is full of joy today
For friends across the ocean foam
Have sent to me good news from home.

> When shall I see the cottage door
> Where I spent years of joy before?
> 'Twas there I knew no grief or care
> My heart was always happy there.
>
> Though I may never see it more
> Nor stand upon my native shore
> Where ere on earth I chance to roam
> My heart will always cling to home.

Today I received the long expected letter from home. I was truly glad to hear from there, and I never cherished the receiving of a letter more than I did this one, but it makes me feel unusually sad. Truly a home has lost all of its quietude and pleasure when surrounded by a cruel and hostile foe. May God permit us to be avenged, even to a small degree, for the insults and mean treatment perpetrated by those cruel vandals of the North. I have hope a day will come when every Northerner will rue the hour when first he set his foot on Virginia's soil. Dire will be the conflict when we meet the foe. Streams of gore may flow around, but not until we free Virginia from the pollution of Northern hordes, will we lay down our arms and cry for peace. That day is near at hand. An avenging God is surely witnessing the affairs of men. Today has been the most disagreeable I have spent. It has been raining since early yesterday morning. A perfect storm has been raging today, so much so that it sometimes required our united exertions to keep our tent from being blown away. The large hospital tent of our Regt. was blown down while it was full of sick. They, however were immediately removed, but not until they were completely drenched. Oh, how much do those sick men need a lady's hand to press their fevered brows. How cheerfully it would be done by their mothers and sisters at home. So common has death become, that when a man dies, he is as soon forgotten. Yesterday I passed by the graveyard of our Regt., it being in a line of the timber which we were felling as a blockade. A few tall hemlock pines were left around them, in respect for the dead. They lie far from the road, in a secluded spot. This may possibly be our fighting ground. The din and clangor of battle may sweep over them, as opposing squadrons meet in terrible combat. But they will sleep on. In that bright sphere their pure souls shall forever stand unmoved during the wreck of time, and crush of worlds.

Saturday, Sept. 28 . . . The air has been extremely cool today, so much so that fire was absolutely indispensable.

Sept. 29 . . . Last night was the coolest of any we have had at this place. The frost was near *ankle deep* in various places. Blankets were very comfortable, but as Mike and Draper were both sick, we had to defer much more to them. This is the Sabbath. I did not know it, however, until quite late in the morning. It is the most serene and beautiful day I have seen for some time. How different it is to the day I spent just one year ago. We have preaching this evening by the Rev.—fighting parson—Crooks. He is 1st Lieut. in Co. I.

Sept. 30 . . . Nothing new today. I wrote a letter this evening to Julia, by Mr. S. There was a skirmish with the pickets today. The nights are extremely cool. I ate some blackberries today.

Oct. 3 . . . I was detailed for grand guard last night. There were a few posts between mine and the enemy. About daylight the farthest pickets commenced firing. A tremendous body of the enemy, drove us all within a mile of camp. We there formed and awaited his approach. He soon came. We were engaged in a brisk fire, when Col. Ramsey of 1st Georgia Regt. came and . . . (Illegible) . . . large body of . . . got between us and the camp . . . we immediately took up the mountain. And now I am sitting beside a log. Am tired of the fight. What with the turn of affairs, now shall I ever write any more in my diary?

Oct. 4 . . . The fight is over. But several of our men are killed. One from our company and two from Capt. Sturms', and about ten killed and missing from our Regt. Nearly all of our loss occurred when checking the advances of the enemy on picket guard. We received the applause of the entire encampment. Some of the officers said that they had never seen more gallantry in pickets—not even in the Mexican war. We were very pleased with their compliments. I did not know that we were in as heavy a fire as we were. The smoke utterly obscured the fight from us. But our friends in camp told us that the clouds of smoke rolled up from the valley like a city was on fire. We kept the whole force of the enemy in check for one hour and a half. Some of our pieces of artillery fired some 93 rounds. Hundreds of our tents are shot through and through with cannon balls. Several horses were shot. Only one man was killed with the cannon shot—he having his head shot off. An Englishman, belonging to our Regt. and was in the French army at the taking of Sebastopol in the Crimean war, was shot while on picket yesterday. He was shot with a large minie rifle ball, directly through the head—the ball entering his face by the side of his nose. I never saw such a corpse.

Saturday, Oct. 5 . . . On picket guard again. Extremely heavy duties have to be performed now. We are on guard every other night. Mr. James Campbell and I are on a post, and neither of us are allowed to sit down or sleep. The penalty for disobeying this martial law is death. We however, sit down, but dare not close our eyes until sent to camp in the morning.

So much exposure and loss of sleep I now sensibly feel, not minding its effect in after life, if I should survive the perils of this warfare.

After the fight on Thursday some of our men went over to the ground occupied by the Yankees. The ground was literally plowed up with our cannon shot. Much blood was seen. Several arms and bones were found along the edge of the field where they had drawn up their infantry. Many canteens and blankets were found. I have a spring socket bayonet. We found several dead. Among others was a young man who more particularly took attention. He was lying by the edge of the forest—having been struck by a cannon ball. His name was Abbott, from an Indiana Regt. In his portmanteau we found three twists of nicely braided hair, from his sisters. He had a furlough for several days. He had written a letter to his sisters saying he would not start home as soon as he expected, as the army was going down the mountain to whip the rebels, and he was going to accompany it so he could tell them about it when he came home. Poor fellow. His furlough was exchanged into a *fur-long*. I have the blues very badly today. Oh how I long to see my friends.

Monday, Oct. 7 . . . This is a gloomy evening. The clouds are hanging around the summits of the distant mountains, and the previous drizzling rain has now changed into torrents. How truly gloomy! Would that I could hope. It is the beautiful tomorrow that may never come. What a life, what a condition for any human being! Often heretofore have I tried to delineate the terrible realities of war, but to one who experiences its manifold terrors, the pen falls from our grasp, and we can only express ourselves to those who like us, have experienced the same. War is surely the results of man's ambitions. How clearly it shows the folly of the human heart. Can we still hope for success? Our country, I fear, is lost, forever is lost to me. Can we still be encouraged to fight for a much loved, but now ruined country?

Tuesday, Oct. 8 . . . On picket guard again. It is going to be intensely cold tonight, especially as I have no blanket, having lost it in the fight. Col. Ramsey offered me one, but I wouldn't accept it.

Sunday, Oct. 13 . . . I have been detailed to assist in the post office for the last few days. I was truly glad of it, for I was tired of so much military duty. We have some famous batteries now. I was informed by our officer Lt. G. T. Thompson, that I would have to go on picket duty again tomorrow, that I was not regularly detailed for the post office duty. They have treated me very badly since I have been in the company. I remember well every insult. A day will surely come when they will rue everything they have done against me. I will be regularly detailed if I can.

I feel extremely lonely this evening. I commenced a letter to Emma a few minutes ago, but the hopelessness of its ever being received caused me to desist. I know she has much trouble concerning me—far more than I have about myself.

> Oh be this warfare of the world accursed.
> The son now weeps not over his father's bier,—
> But gray-haired,—for nature is reversed—
> Drops over his boy's grave an icy tear.

I must quit for tonight. The nights are extremely cold for one who has no blanket or overcoat. I lost mine in the picket skirmish.

Oct. 16 . . . I am now sitting in the office waiting for the mail. I didn't go on picket the other day. I merely paid Mirt Johnson $1 to take my place. But this evening I am detailed again. I don't intend to go if money will hire a substitute. Our P.M. has been sick, and has been at home all day. We mail daily near 800 letters.

A considerable alarm was raised this morning. Our pickets commenced firing—but as it was found out—at our own men, who were just returning from a scout. None were hurt. Our scouts killed three of the enemy. It was a very daring act to go so close to the enemy's camp as to kill some of their pickets, when it was expected they would advance upon our position. I am getting tired of so much foolery. If we have to fight, I wish they would attack us again, and not have so much "bushwacking".

I have formed some very interesting acquaintances since I have been in the post office. It is surprising to see how many intelligent and accomplished young men belong to the Southern Army, and merely privates in the ranks. I am going to visit the South when the war is over.

Oct. 17 . . . I have an invitation to *dine out* tomorrow. Col. Ramsey of the 1st. Georgia Regt. sent an invitation to me to come and see him. It has commenced raining this evening like fury. It is not necessary to say anything about having the blues. I heard today we will winter here. If they attempt that, I will leave sure as fate. The weather is most disagreeable here—damp and cold all the time. Couldn't I enjoy the luxuries of home now! How I would like to go to bed at home on such a rainy evening as this, knowing that I could sleep soundly and be perfectly dry until morning. The most disagreeable thing I can now think of, is to be rained upon at night, when you are very tired and sleepy. I have heard of *swearing* as being characteristic of a soldier,—and he would be very apt to do it then.

Oct. 18 . . . Nothing to say today.

Oct. 24 . . . I am sitting in the Post Office after the mail has come and gone. I was regularly detailed for this business for a period of five days—except this evening. Capt. Bradford came to our company on the 21st. We have an occasional alarm.

Oct. 26 . . . Nothing of importance has transpired in the last few days. I am still in the P.O. Our Regt. is expressing much interest as to the location of winter quarters. I think we should be about due to go back, as no Regt. in the service has undergone more fatigue and labor. We have been in every fuss in the north western part of the state, and when there was any rough work to be done, we did it. I think we will get to comfortable quarters, as our Col. Wm. L. Jackson is doing much for its accomplishment. I received a letter from cousin Betty Butcher last night. They are in New Market, Va.

Oct. 29 . . . I am sitting in the P.O., having been posting bills. Our company has been much more agreeable since our Capt. has returned. He is disposed to accommodate us as much as he can. I hardly know what to say or think, anymore. I even yet, can scarcely realize my circumstances. What have I now to live for? The most flattering anticipations of a bright future, and a successful career in a business life are forever gone. I am wasting my most precious time. I only have one hope or desire to live—on account of my cherished friends at home. For them I only wish to survive, but if I should not ever again meet them, I hope they may think of me only as giving myself for them, and that I glory in it. May the young men hereafter, in the North, think of the responsibilities of making war upon an innocent people who never did them harm, before they embark in such an enterprise again. Is conscience dead? Is reason dumb?

Nov. 6 . . . This is a very disagreeable day. The mountains in the distance are covered with snow. I expect we will have to winter here. If they do keep our Regt. here they will never get another Western Va. volunteer. We have been badly treated. I will have various scores to settle after the war is over.

Nov. 13 . . . I feel like never writing any more. I have quit hoping to ever see our subjugated county as it was once. I feel more like throwing down my gun and cursing the hour I was born to witness such a condition of affairs, than of doing anything else. Unless there is some action soon, I will answer to my name—at a distance! I have a strong idea of getting drunk tonight. I would sure, if it was to be had this side of Yankeedom. Will and Mike are off somewhere on the sick list. I feel somewhat indisposed myself—every time there is a fight on hand! But I have not gone yet! Bud and I console ourselves over a large two-gallon bottle we keep on hand, but which is empty nearly all the time. I wonder if they at home ever think about us. But I wonder more, what they would think if they were to see me with my large vial filled with whiskey!

Nov. 18 . . . Whew! How cold it is this morning! . . . It is now night. We have received marching orders. Our destination is undoubtedly fixed for the top of Allegheny Mountain. Not to save the life of Gen. Loring, and all the sons of bitches in the Confederate Army, would I volunteer again! Not many know where we are going, but I—being a *high private,* find out many things. Bud and I are going to back out in the morning—but not until we get our large bottle filled!

Nov. 19 . . . Bud and I did not leave this morning. The whole of the command is going to leave on the 21st. We sent our baggage this morning. Everything appears the same as when we retreated from Laurel Hill. I dread this winter sure. I expect we will stay on the mountain, unless driven out, ie. our Regt., the 37th, 25th and Hansbrough's battalion. I do not like the place where we will winter. We will have to keep up a strong picket guard all winter. The 44th Va. Regt.—the grandest cowards in the army, are going back over the mountain. Affairs will be different next spring. If ever I again, see J. E. Hall in a muster roll, I will be *tite* when it is put there. A man dies every now and then in our Regt. I felt extremely sorry for one poor fellow who was lying in a tent without any fire. He had the fever, but was suffering greatly from the extreme cold. Sickness is more to be dreaded by far in the army, than the bullets. No bravery can achieve anything against it. The soldier may sicken and die, without receiving any attention but from the rough hands of his fellow soldiers. When buried he is as soon forgotten. Not a stone is raised to tell his living name, age or race. But many a bitter tear is shed over his melancholy fate by kind friends far away. A lady from Ga. came with her husband to see their son in this army. He had died before they came. When I saw her she was weeping bitterly. They planted a white rose over his grave, the only crown of glory received. He lies in a dense pine woods, and the sad melody of the wind as it continually blows through the branches, seems to sing a requiem full of dark forebodings.

Nov. 20 . . . Everything indicates another retreat. The Quarter Master told me that thousands of dollars worth of property—both private and public—would be destroyed. To make things appear a little worse than otherwise would be, I am detailed as one to bring up the rear guard of the army. I expect nothing more than to have a fight of it. Draper and I buried our memento—a cannon ball—of the battle of the 3rd of Oct. We buried it just N. 85° 32″ E; dis. 3 yds. 9¼ in. from a certain chestnut stump, and about 2 rods east of another certain pine tree. We, or either of us will get it during a calmer reign of human affairs. Good night, Dixie. God only knows how we will make our fight tomorrow, if it should be a nasty one.

Nov. 25 . . . We had no fight. If you only knew the discouraging circumstances in which we are placed this morning, I know you would never expect to see us again. We had a most awful march up here through the mud and cold. When we came here we had to lie on the frozen ground without any fire. We have now built a fireplace in our tent, but we have no straw, and a continual vapor is rising from the frozen but now thawing, ground. We have suffered much with the cold. I hope I may stand up against the rigors of the coming winter.

Nov. 27 . . . This is my birthday (21). How differently I am placed now compared with the day last year. Then I was in school in Morgantown—never thinking that such changes could ever have transpired in the history of one's life. I sometimes think I will again enjoy such times, although when I think upon the hardships I have undergone, and the prospect of still harder to come, hope almost dies. Never once did I suppose that in a country like this, a soldier would be so much exposed. Many times the mud has been shoe-top deep in and out of our tents. I was surely reared for a better destiny than this. It is evidently a condition in which God never intended any human being to be placed. One year of my life has passed away —one that could have been of infinite importance to me. At my age, one year is worth three in after life. But instead of being usefully spent, it is in a manner idled away. This is an extremely unpleasant day. The sleet and rain are falling incessantly. I am detailed to help load wagons out in the mountains. We are drawing logs for huts. The huts are not for us —but for the 12th Ga. Regt. How would you like such work?

Nov. 28 . . . Today was tolerably pleasant, but this evening great gusts of sleet and rain are falling. We will have a gay time of it tonight. I was assisting in loading logs on a wagon out in the mountains. I had to be walking about in the snow over my shoe tops, and was nearly frozen from handling the logs. I stood it for an hour or so, and then I told the Lieut. that I would see him in hell a mile, before I would stay any longer. So I came away. I expect he will report me. I was going to ask for a furlough tomorrow to go out to Monterey. I now have some doubts as to my getting it!

Dec. 1 . . . I got the furlough, but did not go. I am going to ask for one in a short time, to go home. Nothing more than usual has transpired in the last three days. The cooking department is beginning to lag again. I don't like to eat nothing but beef! Sometimes we have eaten it after holding it before the fire with a stick, and then eat off it as it cooked—having it mixed with plenty of blood. It takes a month's wages to buy anything now. I will give some prices:

Cheese	75 cents per lb.
Butter	35-40
Apples	50 per doz. or $5 per bu.
Apple butter	25 per pt.
Cabbage	25 per head
Chicken	50
Potatoes	$4 per bu.
Whiskey	$20.00 per gal.

Dec. 5 . . . I have been sick during the last 4 days. How I would like to have Ma's tender care.

Dec. 14 . . . Yesterday we had another heavy fight. (Note: Battle of Camp Allegheny, Federals defeated with loss of 137 killed and wounded.)

Early yesterday morning—4 o'clock—Lieut. G. T. Thompson roused us up and formed the company. After a few minutes we were marched out on the hill with the remainder of the Regt. We almost froze while standing in the piercing wind. About sunrise a flanking party commenced firing on our rear. We immediately deployed to the right, and engaged the enemy, who were stationed in the edge of the woods. We suffered much—the enemy having decidedly the advantage, being in the woods,—with us in the open field, and having the sun shining full in our faces. Our men fought under these disadvantages for near 3½ hours. Some of our best men fell—some for whom I had the strongest regard. Our Regt. was at last nearly surrounded, and had to retreat. Most of the Regt. fell back to the battery and trenches. The fight still continued for several hours. Capt. P. B. Anderson, the hero of 50 battles, was slain. The enemy at last retreated. We found a great many of the enemy lying on the field after the fight. I cannot exult over our victory. Such work is a shock to human nature. We lost too many brave men to rejoice over our victory.

Dec. 15 . . . Affairs are tolerably quiet. Some of our wounded men are dying occasionally. This is the Sabbath. On this day twelve months ago I arrived home from Morgantown. How little did I think my condition would be so changed—I have seen enough of war. O my God, how forcibly it illustrates the folly and depravity of the human heart. Many of our men suffered intensely of their wounds before they died. Many were groaning from extreme pain, with the cold, clammy sweat of death upon their brows. I hope never to witness such scenes again. I was particularly distressed with the sad fate of my esteemed friend John Nutter, 1st Sgt. in Co. C. Early in the battle I saw him raise his hands and fall. I hurried to his side, but saw he must soon die. I spoke to him, but he could only raise his eyes and smile a faint recognition. He asked very faintly for water, but I could not tarry longer with him. We hurried over here in the wild excitement of the hour, and left him there to die alone. When I saw him again he was dead. The vital current had ceased to flow, and a hitherto warm and faithful heart was forever cold and still.

Dec. 18 . . . We are expecting another attack. I have been working on some batteries today. We have to sleep with our arms and accouterments fixed. I do hope Heaven may stop the further effusion of blood.

Dec. 25 . . . 1861. This is Christmas, and as is common there must be some amusement and festivities going on. We are *amusing* ourselves hovering around a fire in our tent, which smokes us nearly to death. Though last night was Christmas Eve, I did not sleighride much! Instead of that, we were marched out with the Regt. on the mountain, to guard the batteries and artillery. We spent our Christmas Eve very gaily, sure. We are still living in our tents, but we make them tolerably comfortable by constructing rude fireplaces to them. At night we do not fare so well. Some mornings when we awaken our blankets are wet with frost, and the inside of our tent lined with hoar frost. Many times our hair is frozen stiff by congealed respiration, and our floor is covered with snow. This is a pleasant life, sure. I was at home this time one year ago.

Dec. 27 . . . I was on camp duty last night. The night was quite cold. I will spend my holidays differently next year. I am going to *bake* some *pies* today. Our commanders are getting to be tolerably good to us now. The reason is that during next month we will be asked to reenlist again. We will get $50 and 60 days furlough if we enlist again. I may do it, but, I expect to serve out my time, and then I will be *sure* of a furlough.

Dec. 29 . . . I have come to the conclusion not to volunteer again. Our officers have not given us any encouragement to do so. We have had but one continual scene of hardship compared with other troops. We have had duties to perform which no other regiment in this brigade has performed. I am resolved never to be enrolled again. Ever since Sept. every Co. in the Regt. has assisted in building cabins, but they are all now occupied by others, and we are still in our tents. As far as cooking utensils are concerned, we have not been furnished with anything but one bucket. I am so extremely tired of camp life. I long so much to enjoy the pleasures of society. Here, nothing but a collected mass of human beings are assembled, who have lost all of those finer feelings which makes a man a man, caused by the recklessness of life, and the continual connection with the immediate scenes of death. It is horrible to anyone not used to it, to hear the blasphemies of the soldiers. I know there is an apparent special Providence directing the affairs of our country, and over every battle field. His care seems to be doubly manifest, but I could not wonder if He should turn against us—seeing so much wickedness.

Dec. 31 . . . "The old year has gone, and with it many a thought of happy dreams." It has also closed the scenes of many of the darkest periods of history. What great events may transpire in the coming year! A nation will doubtless realize a name and status among other nations of the earth. The United States will rank with the mighty dead—numbered with the fallen greatness of Troy, Greece and Rome. She will then have ceased to exist, but has merely followed the examples of all overthrown Governments. Future ages may read of her greatness and grandeur, but the glory of her arms, and the magnificence of her institutions will forever live in song.

1862

Jan. 3, 1862 . . . I was on picket last night. The air snowed frost all night. An alarm was given last night, and we were told to prepare ourselves to fight near 10,000 of the enemy, who were advancing upon us, and were only about 8 or 9 miles off.

Sunday, Jan. 5 . . . This is one of the most peculiar days I ever saw. We are in the midst of the clouds, and frost has been falling all day. It must be about two inches deep. The trees are covered with it, and the small tendrils are wonderfully magnified. Nice times for men to live in tents.

Jan. 7 . . . Winter is now coming in earnest. I never experienced colder weather. We are still living in our tents. The fireplaces we have constructed do tolerably well while the fire lasts, but at night we suffer considerably, until the snow blows over us enough to cover us, when we sleep quite well. We retire about ten o'clock at night, and get at from 11 to 1 next day. Nothing of interest has transpired of late in the army. We still have an occasional alarm.

Jan. 14 . . . This is an extremely wintry morning. We are still in tents, but some of the company are going to move into huts today. We only have 2 cabins, and there will be 18 in each. Cousin Will, Mike, Draper and I, respectfully declined going into one. Four months from today and we will be out of this accursed war. If they never retake Western Virginia, I will say goodbye to Dixie forever.

Jan. 22 . . . I have heard bad news from home—that uncle James had died on the 31st of Dec. '61. Oh what has befallen our once quiet and peaceful community! Will our country ever be freed from the curses of such a war. If I volunteer again, I will never join the North Western Army, but will operate on the Eastern or Southern Coast.

Jan. 27 . . . I received three letters from home this morning. I was truly glad to hear from them, but a peculiar sadness seems to fill me tonight. Oh, is our country forever lost? Shall our friends forever be in a land of such oppression! What changes have transpired in our history! Truly man is a creature of change. From the earliest dawn of his existence down to the hour of dissolution, mutation is linked with his destiny.

Feb. 5 . . . We have gone into the pie business of late. We bake about one dozen a day, which we sell at $3.25 a piece.

Feb. 7 . . . Nothing of interest has transpired of late. We daily go through with the same routine of passing away time. We have to get up every morning at daylight to roll call. We have to attend, regardless of the most disagreeable weather. The pie business is still flourishing. I have been commencing a diary of a letter home.

Feb. 12 . . . A considerable snowstorm has been blowing over the mountain last night and today. The air is about as cold as they make it. All things are quiet. We heard that our forces were defeated again, now at Roanoke Island. I hope however it is not as bad as reported. An opportunity was presented today for us to re-enlist. I did not accept.

Feb. 13 . . . Nothing new today. A detachment of men are going down on Greenbrier tonight on a scout.

Feb. 14 . . . On the 14th of next May I will be out of the army—only three months. I am on camp guard today.

Feb. 17 . . . Nothing new has transpired in the last few days. The same old duties of getting wood, etc. to be performed every day. I am getting most darn tired of this infernal war.

Feb. 27, midnight . . . We were marched to the ditches tonight about 7 o'clock, and remained until eleven. The trenches had lots of snow in them, the ground frozen perfectly hard, and the wind singing like minie balls. After we learned no enemy was coming we marched back to our quarters almost chilled to death.

Feb. 28 . . . Today was our muster day,—it being the last day of the winter campaign. We all had our muskets shining very brightly indeed. We will soon receive our pay for four months' service.

March 1 . . . Nothing of importance has transpired today. A very nice and pleasant day.

March 2 . . . Snowing, sleeting, raining and blowing all day; the Sabbath. I have forgotten all about "resting one day in seven".

March 4 . . . In a cabin in 44th Regt. Va.

March 5 . . . At Mr. Simmons on the South Branch. Jap and I stayed here one night before on the memorable retreat from Laurel Hill.

March 16, Sunday . . . This is surely a most gloomy time. The Confederacy is in much danger. We are rather expecting a march from this place—also expecting another battle. A very disagreeable day. Sleeting, snow, ground very muddy.

March 22 . . . On camp guard last night. Nothing new. Some few discharges of artillery were heard this morning at some far off camp. We are looking for some busy times here now in a few days. Going home next May if there is no danger of the enemy capturing me.

March 23 . . . Affairs are still quiet. Got a letter from Will today. Still sick. No news.

March 24 . . . All right today. I received two letters from Barbour this evening—from two of my *lady* friends.

March 26 . . . Affairs are quiet yet. Some think we will have to fall farther back and abandon our present position. I do hope we will not.

March 28 . . . Many gloomy apprehensions are entertained about our evacuating this post. We were reinforced today by the Highland and Pocahontas Militia.

March 30, Sunday . . . On picket guard today—away down a ravine on the side of the mountain next to the enemy. Everything indicates a backward movement of this command.

April 1 . . . We have struck our tents and loaded our baggage for a march. Two days rations cooked.

April 2 . . . We commenced to march this morning at about ten o'clock. We marched to Monterey — 16 miles. A very disagreeable march.

April 3 . . . Left Monterey this morning and marched to McDowell, a distance of 10 miles. We are camped in a beautiful valley. All the soldiers are in good spirits, but Western Virginians think it looks but little like getting home. Mike lost his pocketbook containing $70 this morning.

April 4 . . . We are still encamped at McDow-

ell. Drilled some today.
. . . .

May 18 . . . (My diary is continued from Book I) Many eventful scenes have transpired since anything was written in my former book. A detailed narrative is sufficient to illustrate everything. We left our encampment at McDowell early on the morning of the 5th of April, and marched about 12 miles to the eastern side of the Shenandoah mountain, where we encamped.

April 6 . . . Still remaining at Shenandoah.

April 7 . . . Recd. a letter from Cousin Will.

April 8 . . . A very disagreeable day. The snow was about 4 inches deep.

April 9 . . . A very miserable time indeed. It appears as if winter were just commencing. We had to either freeze or smoke ourselves nearly to death around our log fires out in the snow, rain and sleet. Heard of a fight in Corinth, Miss.

April 10 . . . Nothing new today.

April 13 . . . On camp guard. Nothing of importance has happened in the last 3 days.

April 14 . . . It is now one month from the time we have thought we would be out of this delightful war. How anxiously we looked for that much wished for period. A change, however, came over the spirit of my dreams.

April 15 . . . All quiet today.

April 16... We received tolerably doleful news. Our company was paraded and every man mustered into service for the war. No difference whether we reenlisted or not. A considerable damper on our future prospects and expectations. We grumbled about the government doing us injustice, and will continue to do so.

April 17 . . . Somewhat cast down today on account of the affairs which transpired yesterday. There was an alarm about noon, and we were all marched off to the mountain, but returned when it was ascertained no enemy was coming.

April 19 . . . We received marching orders and started at 2 o'clock. Camped about midnight on the western base of Calf Mountain.

April 20, Easter . . . marched within 6 miles of Staunton. Awful marching. Almost died this evening.

April 21 . . . Still encamped at Valley. . . . Rain all day. No tents nor much to eat.

April 25 . . . Nothing but rain and snow for several days. Oh what dismal times. How gloomy.

April 27, The Sabbath. Went to church. The first time an opportunity has presented itself since last fall. A beautiful day.

May 1 . . . We elected our regimental and company officers today. G. T. Thompson, I. V. Johnson, M. M. Rider are our company Commissioned Officers.

May 2 . . . Left our camp early to go on a scout. Went to the western side of Buffalo Mountain. Saw none of the enemy. Returned to Buffalo Gap and remained all night. Relieved next morning by 3 companies of the 44th Va. Regt.

May 3 . . . Returned to camp near 12 o'clock. Had a brigade dress parade. Rumor afloat of a move on hand.

May 6 . . . Nothing new . . . Expect to leave here soon and go somewhere—to what point, God only knows. Heard today of the death of my friends Col. Parsons and his daughter Miss Kate. They were driven from home by our common enemy the Federals. We started from our camp today about 12 o'clock. Marched to the summit of Buffalo Mountain.

May 7 . . . Started early this morning and marched to the western side of Shenandoah Mountain. The enemy held the top of the Mountain, but fled without any resistance. A considerable picket fight occurred as we approached the mountain. The enemy lost two men killed, two prisoners, and 3 horses. We lost none. As we approached the ravines on the western side of the mountain, the enemy opened up on us with a 12 pounder rifle cannon. They did no execution more than to arrest our advance until morning.

May 8 . . . Started at an early hour. Col.

Baldwin's Brigade in front today. Ours next (Col. Conner's). We then ascertained several more Regts. had come to assist us. The whole force was as follows: Va. Regts. 2nd, 3rd, 4th, 5th, 10th, 20th, 21st, 23rd, 25th, 27th, 31st, 33rd, 37th, 42nd, 44th, 48th, 52nd, 58th, and the 12th Ga. Regt. One Regt. of cavalry, and near 40 pieces of artillery. We soon found that the enemy was stationed at McDowell. As we ascended Bull Mountain, the heavy sound of artillery told us only too plainly that the enemy was going to give us battle. We halted on top of the mountain, and expected to remain there all night, and then attack the enemy next morning. Six or seven men were sent from each company down the mountain to cook for the remainder. I was among the number that was sent. About sunset that evening, to our surprise, the heavy and incessant roll of musketry told us the battle had actually begun. In a few moments the wounded were coming in ambulances in great numbers. What few houses were there, were soon filled, and tents were pitched for the accommodation of others. It was a sorrowful sight to hear the groans of these poor men. Among many others of my acquaintance that were seriously wounded was my cousin Doctor Armstrong, Assistant Surgeon of the 25th Va. Regt. I got permission of my Capt. to stay and wait on him until he should leave for a hospital. Our troops were victorious, and early next morning started in pursuit of the fleeing enemy. Much baggage and commissary stores were taken. Much commissary goods the enemy burned.

May 9 . . . I remained with Dr. Armstrong all day. He was badly wounded.

May 10 . . . Dr. A. started to Staunton today, and I therefore went to join my Regt. I crossed the battlefield as I went. The ground was literally torn up by the balls, and in some places not even a twig of the bushes was untouched. I next visited the camp of the enemy. Heaps of tents and cooking utensils lay all around. Soon after I left there I came to a large caisson in the pike. Nearly all the shot had been removed. A few spherical case and conical shells still remained. Stayed all night within 5 miles of the army after a hard walk.

May 11 . . . Started next morning and overtook the army a few miles from Franklin. Remained all that night and suffered considerably from the cold chilly air.

May 12 . . . Left our present position about 12 o'clock and marched back to S. a distance of 7 miles.

May 13 . . . Started this morning about ten o'clock and marched to the "Forks of Waters" about 10 miles.

May 14 . . . Started again at daylight. My

shoes, that had given out about the time that I overtook the army, could not be mended any more. As a matter of course I had to go it without. Marched today 18 miles, and to make it more disagreeable it rained all day. Encamped on the western base of Shenandoah mountain.

May 15 . . . Still raining. Tried to get permission to ride, but could not. Marched about 15 miles and encamped somewhere—has no name, nor never should have—on the road leading to Harrisonburg.

May 16 . . . Still at the same place. None of us have tents, and the rain has never ceased. Our time,—or the time for which we enlisted, expired yesterday.

May 17 . . . Started very early this morning. Marched to Bridgewater, Rockingham County. Nearly used up after so much barefoot marching.

May 18 . . . Still encamped near Bridgewater. A beautiful country here. I am awfully tired of war. I can not keep from feeling sad when I look around over this fruitful country, and see nature smiling in luxuriance, "as if the war demon still slumbered, or stalked only through his accustomed haunts beyond the ocean",—and then to meditate upon the probability of this beautiful valley soon being overrun by our vandal foes. Our camp is on a slight eminence, and the scene is truly romantic.

May 19 . . . Left our camp at Bridgewater this morning at 7 o'clock, and marched about 2 miles beyond Harrisonburg. The roads are in good order.

May 20 . . . Now encamped on the Staunton and Winchester pike, a short distance above New Market. We are very much wearied by the march, in fact, virtually worn down. A night's rest appears to do us no good—just as sleepy and languid in the morning as when we stop in the evening. We passed several deserted camps of the enemy today. They have almost ruined the county about here. The air is so soft and mellow that it forcibly reminds me of those beautiful days when I used to wander over the blue hills of home.

May 21 . . . Left our camp at New Market this morning, and marched to the eastern side of Massanutten Mountain. We have orders to cook 2 days' rations and be ready to march by 5 in the morning. After marching all day—having to be up cooking half the night. Another fight is surely pending. Some Louisianians passed us today.

May 22 . . . Now encamped on the pike leading to Front Royal today. Fired our guns off this evening. Almost tired to death.

May 23 . . . Our advance had a considerable skirmish with the enemy at Front Royal today.

Lots of prisoners were taken and the enemy wholly routed. We encamped 2 miles north of town.

May 24 . . . Marched a mile or two along the road, and halted to await orders. Cannonading can be distinctly heard in the direction of Winchester and Strasburg. Gen. Ashby's cavalry is continually bringing in prisoners. About 2 o'clock we started at a brisk pace for Middletown on the road between Strasburg and Winchester. When we got there a great line of Yankee prisoners were guarded by the roadside, and dead horses were lying all around. We marched on that night and encamped within 6 miles of Winchester. We had hardly built our fires before we had to "fall in" again. We marched within 2 miles of Winchester. Went to sleep several times marching along. We stopped by the roadside and waited until morning.

May 25 . . . At the earliest dawn of morning the cannonading commenced on our advance. We marched forward until we had a splendid view of the fight. The cannonading was tremendous. In a short time the enemy commenced retreating, and in doing so set the town on fire. We rushed through the town amid the cheers and congratulations of the citizens, and the cracking and burning houses. We pursued the enemy about 5 miles. Vast amounts of stores were captured by our troops.

May 26 . . . Our brigade marched back through town and camped about 2 miles above.

May 27 . . . Still at the same place.

May 28 . . . Had orders to march today in the shortest kind of time. Marched until ten at night, and camped 12 miles from Charles Town. Our company was sent out on picket, but had to report at 2 o'clock next morning.

May 29 . . . Started very early and marched 2 miles beyond Charles Town. Heavy cannonading heard in Harpers Ferry.

May 30 . . . Started about noon for Harpers Ferry, went another two miles and "about faced", and to our surprise, marched nearly to Winchester, a distance of 25 miles. About midnight the rain fell in perfect torrents. We could not lie down, although many did.

May 31 . . . Struck out this morning and marched way above Middletown.

June 16 . . . Now encamped near West Meridian, Rockingham Co. Since writing last many eventful scenes have transpired—many of which will be recorded on the pages of our national history. Several skirmishes took place between Strasburg and Harrisonburg. At Harrisonburg Gen. Ashby's cavalry attacked, and drove them through the city, although the victory was dearly bought. Gen. Ashby being slain the next day, June 6, everything was tolerably quiet. Our army was then only about

6 miles from Harrisonburg, in the direction of Port Republic. On June 7 we were awakened about 2 o'clock in the morning and ordered to cook one day's rations immediately, but before we could commence, everything had to be put in the wagon. About daylight we were marched back about 300 yards, and formed a line of battle. We remained in line all that day—having momentarily expected the enemy to make his appearance. We camped near the same place. Next morning we were marched a few hundred yards farther back. In the meantime, battery after battery and Regt. after Regt. having passed us to the front. The battle soon began. We were hurried farther forward and took a position in the rear of some of the batteries. The cannonading was the most terrific I ever heard. We remained as silent and quiet as if inanimate, for some time, while the cannon balls like winged devils were flying around us. I noticed the countenance of the men. Some looked pale but calm, their eyes tranquil. The knitted brow and flashing eyes of others, showed the more fiery spirit within. We remained in this position, occasionally moving around to the right or left. About 2 o'clock Lieut. Whitely of our company was killed— shot through the head. That night we camped near the battle field. The next morning the heavy roll of cannon in the direction of Port

Republic announced the enemy approach in this direction. Our whole army moved, and attacked him. The fight lasted for 3 or 4 hours. Our Regt. lost many men. The enemy at last retreated, and was pursued for many miles. Our command started as if going across Blue Ridge, but remained on the western side 2 days, and then moved down and camped near West Meridian. We remained there until the 17th, when we were ordered to travel. We marched not far from the Blue Ridge that night and encamped.

June 18 . . . Started at an early hour and marched over the mountain, and camped on the Mechums River.

June 19 . . . Marched from the river to . . . . The day was excessively hot.

June 20 . . . Still at Charlottesville. A most beautiful day. The calmest and most serene day that I have seen for a long time. We all are much puzzled by this movement of the army. What it means, none can form the slightest conjecture. May abandon Virginia. May be a pitched fight.

June 21 . . . Left Charlottesville and marched to Gordonsville. Elected 3rd Lieut. today.

June 22 . . . The Sabbath. Left Gordonsville today—on a train—the first one we have ridden for a long time. Now encamped near Louisa Court House. Stay all night, we expect.

June 24 . . . Left Louisa C.H. this morning

and rode in the cars to Beaver Dam, a distance of 24 miles. Have a headache today. Left Beaver Dam at 2 o'clock, and marched 15 miles in the direction of the enemy.

June 25 . . . Started very early and marched to Ashland.

June 26 . . . Left Ashland and marched to the first position of the enemy, who completely gave way before the advance of our army.

June 27 . . . Stayed with the Regiment no longer. Left sick, but started next morning with W. B. Holt of the Regt. We came to the edge of the army about night, but could not find where our Regt. or Brigade had gone. Laid down. The firing of artillery was brisk, but the rolling of musketry surpassed anything I ever heard—one continuous roar.

June 28 . . . Can learn nothing about the location of our Regt.

June 29 . . . Passed over part of the battlefield today. Saw a few dead Yankees. Some were as black in the face as the Ace of Spades. Let lie and rot, I expect. This is the Sabbath. I am awfully tired of this kind of life. Not changed clothes for a month, nor much prospect of doing so very soon.

July 4 . . . We have been marching all day, but I am lost as to the country about here. Damn such a way of spending the Fourth. I am so awfully tired of war I hardly know what to do.

July 13 . . . Now in Richmond. Sent here to a hospital. This is the Sabbath. One among the most beautiful days I ever beheld. I did not go to church for various reasons—(my ailment) The music of the organ sounds beautifully to the ear. I am staying at a common boarding house near the Capitol. I have a strong notion of quitting my diary. Everything is engraved on my memory—no need of having events recur. I may however write more, but it will be as a mere pastime.

Aug. 7 . . . Now at White Sulphur at a hospital. A nice place under any other circumstances than the present.

Aug. 8 . . . I have an idea of leaving here soon. I don't like the idea of staying here where fashion and . . . still exist to some . . . is a perfect hell to . . . .

Aug. 17 . . . Now at Lynchburg. Left the Springs on the 11th, and came to this place the same day. Obtained permission to visit my uncle at Buckingham Court House, but could not leave before the evening of the 13th. At 5 P.M. I got aboard the "Jeff Davis" and started. Arrived at Hardwicksville on the morning of the 14th, and started on foot for Maysville. Arrived there about noon the same day—had a glorious time with my relations—many of whom I had not seen for 15 months. The nice times I used to have at home were fully brought to my mind. I almost fancied I was at home. Left there the morning of the 16th and went to Hardwicksville, and took the boat again for this city. Will leave in the morning—the 18th —for Gordonsville and will . . . (illegible) . . . I dread the hell fired marches we will have to undergo. I am in a dismal scrape now, and if I ever get out, I will be more careful what part of the service I will enter again.

Sept. 22 . . . Rather be in hell than here in this cursed army. Going to get out of it soon by some means.

Sept. 27 . . . Bunker Hill.

Oct. 11, 1862 . . . The army is encamped at this time 12 miles from Winchester on the northern side. We have been here for several days. Considerable duty has to be performed now. I am on camp guard today. Went down and tore up the Railroad and came back and encamped about 2 miles from the old position. We left here on the morning of . . . and in the P.M. encamped a few miles from Berryville. Left our camp there in the morning of . . . and stopped at Millwood. We only remained there until the . . . when we took up a new camp at White Post. On the morning of . . . we left our camp and marched in the direction of Front Royal. The Brigade encamped about 5 miles from the same place, but our Regt. went in sight, to act as picket during the night. Early the next morning the Brigade passed us, going on to tear up the R.R. Our Regt. went back and camped on the position which the Brigade had occupied. On the 11th of Nov. the Brigade returned. We remained there until the 13th, when we moved our position about two miles.

Nov. 15 . . . We received orders last night to cook two days' rations and march this morning to the Shenandoah River, which we crossed about noon. We are now encamped on the Manassas R.R. in the Manassas Gap, and about 6 miles from the river. Nights are extremely cool.

Nov. 16 . . . After a hard day's work tearing up the R.R.'s, we are now encamped where we were last night. Our rations were out this evening, but can not draw any until tomorrow. I went about 1/2 miles and got some corn.

Nov. 17 . . . Returned to camp today and cooked our rations, as we were nearly starved—had to roast hard corn.

Nov. 18 . . . On picket guard today, near Front Royal. Awful, gloomy day.

Nov. 19 . . . Returned to camp today. Ordered to cook 1 day's rations and be ready to march at daylight.

Nov. 20 . . . Marched to Strasburg—23 miles.

Nov. 21 . . . Marched to Mt. Jackson.

Nov. 22 . . . Marched to the east side of the peaked mountain—21 miles.

Nov. 23 ... Marched to the eastern base of the Blue Ridge—22 miles.

Nov. 24 ... Marched to Madison C.H., a distance of 16 miles.

Nov. 25 ... Still at the same place.

Nov. 26 ... No move yet, many conjectures as to where we are going.

Dec. 17 ... Many events have happened since the above was written. We left our camp at Madison C.H. and marched within 15 miles of Fredericksburg on the river below. Our Regt. went on picket while there. Had a long talk with the Yankees, as their pickets were on one side of the river and ours on the other. On the 12th of Dec. we left camp and marched in the direction of Fredericksburg. Very heavy and rapid cannonading was heard for two days before. Dec. 13 left our camp, which was about 4 miles from the ferry, at an early hour, and marched in the direction of the river. About 9 o'clock the enemy opened up on us with artillery. About noon the fight became awful. Our brigade charged through two or three brigades, and attacked the enemy with heavy firing. The enemy was repulsed. Two men were wounded in my company. During the 14th and 15th the two armies were lying within a few hundred yards of each other. During the night of the 15th the enemy recrossed the river. When they went, no one knew. Loud and prolonged cheers were heard on all sides when it was ascertained they had fled. In a few minutes our command commenced its march down the river. We marched to our old camp, and were ordered to cook one day's rations and be ready to march at daylight. We had just gotten our fires built, and had just laid down to rest when we were ordered to "fall in" and go on. We marched on to within about 4 miles of Port Royal where we are now encamped. Had nothing to eat until about 9 this morning. We are expecting to leave here every moment, as it is rumored in the ranks that the enemy is attempting to cross the river near this place.

1863

Jan. 2, 1863 . . . Now encamped about 1 mile from Port Royal. Everything indicates a calm for some time. We have fixed up chimneys in our fly tents. Yesterday was New Year's. Spent my time in building a fireplace. Today we had chicken and potatoes. Chickens cost $1.75 and potatoes $5.00. These are hellish times.

Jan. 4, Sunday . . . The Regt. went out on picket today, but I being a little indisposed, remained in camp. This is a very pleasant day, but most awful gloomy, as are nearly all the other days of my life while in this cursed place.

Feb. 2 . . . Still at the same camp.

Feb. 6, '63 . . . No change in affairs yet. The same old regular routine of duty to be performed. I do not know what will become of me if there is no change soon. I am so tired, tired, tired of this life. Anxiety about home and their unprotected condition among the enemy is enough to make the hours glide slowly away. Will I ever meet with my friends around the social board again? Yes, will I ever!

Feb. 10 . . . Nothing of importance yet. Some heavy cannonading heard up the river.

Feb. 15 . . . This is the Sabbath. But it is a gloomy and cheerless day. The fog has utterly obscured distant objects, and the blue haze that usually girts the horizon, has given place to wintry looking clouds. Heavy duties have to be performed now. On the 13th the Regt. went on fatigue. It marched about 15 miles, and remained making roads until yesterday. It was a dreadful march coming to camp. The average depth of the mud was 5 inches. When we got to camp there was no complaint! But anyone could see in the dull eye, the pale cheek, and languid, travel-worn aspects the hardships all had undergone. No hopes are entertained for this war to end, at least while we live. Great men, to whom existence is not yet given may cast a backward glance upon us *as a people,* and think properly there is something more in war than a poetical representation.

Feb. 17 . . . Snowed hard all day and is keeping on tonight. We are up cooking 4 days' rations to go on picket tomorrow morning. Some little difficulty depending on the light loaf question, as the yeast rising, or whatever it is, is not as prompt as usual. We have to go to the river.

Feb. 18 . . . Got done cooking and got to the river about noon.

Feb. 19 . . . A hard night last night was on the poor soldiers, rained and sleeted all night.

Got perfectly wet. Our fires all rained out, and we suffered much.

Feb. 23 . . . Now in camp. A dismal snowstorm has been blowing over this sandy waste for a few days past. Very disagreeable times. We carry our wood about a quarter of a mile. The 4th Corps left for Newport News on the 23rd. All quiet. The first furloughs granted our company were on the 18th.

March 2 . . . Nothing worthy of note up to this date. The snow has all left and most beautiful weather has taken its place. Orders came today to be ready to march at four o'clock tomorrow morning. Reveille at two. We expect our destination is Fredericksburg. It is only a supposition however. I am now detailed to accompany the wagons and assist them in passing over the heavy roads.

March 5 . . . Now encamped near Fredericksburg. The command arrived here on the evening of the 3rd. It was a march of unusual severity. We took the camp of some troops that had gone to the Southern coast. We occupy the immediate vicinity of the recent battle. An accident occurred on the day we arrived, by some of the boys building a fire on a bomb shell.

March 7 . . . "All quiet along the lines" at this time. On yesterday a man was publicly punished by whipping before the Regt.—it was for violation of the 52nd Act of War. It seemed barbarous and inhuman. God never made a man to be treated so. He will also have to work on the Fortifications around our Capitol for 12 months, with a 24 lb. ball and chain to his leg.

March 9 . . . A beautiful day. We have a Brigade Inspection today.

March 13 . . . Received 2 letters from home yesterday. No news or changes yet.

March 20 . . . A snow storm has been in progress for several days past. On the 18th we were ordered to prepare ourselves to march at a moment's notice, and very far up the river very heavy cannonading was heard at the same time . . . it proved to be a raid of the enemy's cavalry, but the cavalry of our army was sufficient to repel them without the assistance of any infantry. We are expecting to have a fight here in a few days that will require infantry force. W. F. Holt returned to our company to pay us a visit yesterday evening. Having been in the northwest during his absence, he told us much about our friends in that section which we never knew before. I would love to have seen some of the things he represents to have seen.

March 22 . . . All the mess, in fact, all the company, have been on a drunk for the last two days, excepting myself, as I haven't touched a drop, and don't expect to. All the boys are looking beautiful lying around in the dirt. Heretofore I have been temperate, but after seeing the boys on this spree, I have sworn an "eternal abstinence."

March 31 . . . Tomorrow commences our regular spring campaign. All the extra baggage has been sent off, and the troops left in light marching order. I expect we would have gone before this time, if a snow storm had not interfered. No ideas are entertained as to our destination, and neither do we care, for we could not get into a worse place this side of hell, than the present camp. Nothing to eat now days except sour bread and bacon, which is old enough to speak for itself. I have become so tired of it I can hardly eat it at all. We manage to eat one meal of it every other day—when, as a matter of course we are nearly starved.

April 3 . . . A cold, dry day, just in unison with my feelings. No prospect of a move yet. I heard today that a certain number of men out of every Regt. in the service will be received to man our vessels of war, and also for the English expeditions. I hope to God it is only so, for I have already made some arrangements for my being received if the call is ever made. I don't expect to have an easier time in the Navy than I have here, but I can't have a worse time, even if I were in hell. All hope for a more peaceful life to come is almost gone. Hope is the most potent blessing God gave to man, for it will cheer him in the intense gloom of this cruel world, when all other agencies have passed away. When gloom settles upon the mind and darkness shrouds the soul, hope will then be kindled, if the flame is not forever extinct, and the anguish of today is forgotten—in what? The *promised* gladness of tomorrow. Such is hope. Though its ideal imaginations of the future are never realized, it lends a kindly hand to the present hour, and if sustained, will forever banish that terrible word—despair.

April 5, 1863, Easter Sunday . . . The snow is three or four inches deep on the ground, and is still continuing. The Regt. has to go down to Fredericksburg on picket this morning. It is bad weather to start out on a 2 days' picket. No eggs for this Easter!

April 6 . . . Bought some eggs this morning after all, but paid $2.50 per doz.

April 8 . . . Returned to camp yesterday. Nothing new. I, with many others, have symptoms of scurvy. Our mouths are very sore. Very cold weather now.

April 10 . . . Received orders to be ready to march at 12 o'clock. Got aboard a train and started to Gen. Imboden's Command at Shenandoah Mountain.

Apr. 11 . . . Arrived at Staunton this evening and came out of town about 2 miles to camp.

Apr. 12 . . . Still at same place.

Apr. 13 . . . Started this morning at an early

hour and marched to Shenandoah Mt. Arrived there at 3 o'clock.

Apr. 14 . . . At the same camp.

Apr. 15 . . . Started at daylight and marched across the Mt. and "about faced", came back over the mountain, and encamped about 2 miles from the camp we left this morning.

Apr. 16 . . . Still at same place. Expect to leave any moment.

Apr. 19 . . . Sunday. Received orders to cook rations and be ready to march tomorrow morning at 4 o'clock. I expect we will cross the Shenandoah Mountain again for the 6th time. Beautiful weather now. The air feels very soft and balmy, and the little flowers are beginning to peep through the ground to hail with joy the coming of their fair Mistress—Spring. These blue mountains look as though they were welcoming me back again to my native county, and remind me very forcibly of the retired, *free,* and simple life that is led by the hardy mountaineers. But the tramp of the war steed is heard in those valleys, and at early morn a thousand echoes are awakened by the roll of the drum. O, peace, when wilt thou reign again?

April 20 . . . Marched to McDowell. Rained nearly all day.

April 21 . . . Marched to Hightown. Nice marching today. At this point our command formed a junction with Brig. Gen. Wm. L.

Jackson's forces. We do not yet know the extent of his command.

April 22 . . . Marched to Greenbrier River. A Division of the Confederate forces occupied this position at the beginning of the war. The Regt. to which I belong formed a part. Here on the 3rd of Oct. 1861 was the battle of Greenbrier River fought. The casualties on either side were not very great considering the forces engaged. The Federals were defeated. A very different scenery is presented to the eye now, compared to the way it was when occupied by the troops. The hard, baked earth has given way to luxurious vegetation, and all over that broad camp a dead silence reigns, following the hum and stir of busy camp life. The graves of our soldiers who fell in that battle are all sodded over, and the green grass waves in beauty over those fallen heroes, as if it were enjoying the genial air of spring. As we stood around their graves we could almost envy their quiet, peaceful lot, when we remembered what all we had undergone, between that time and the present, and also thought of the probability of a still harder life to come.

Apr. 23 . . . Today we marched to the western base of Cheat Mountain. A very long and weary march.

April 24 . . . Today we marched a few miles west of Beverly. In the morning a foraging train of the enemy's was captured, and when we arrived at Beverly, a brisk skirmish took place between our advance and about 1500 of the enemy, who occupied the town. They soon fled, and we pursued them a few miles, and camped.

April 25 . . . Marched over Rich mountain and encamped.

Apr. 26 . . . Marched within a few miles of Buckhannon river and camped.

Apr. 27 . . . Counter marched today and camped at the same camp we left 2 nights before.

Apr. 28 . . . Marched within 4 miles of Buckhannon town.

Apr. 29 . . . Marched to the town and encamped.

April 30 . . . Still at the same place. Met with my cousin M. E. Taft in town.

May 1 . . . No news yet.

May 2 . . . Started this morning at an early hour. Marched within 4 miles of Weston. The march though short, was fatiguing.

May 3 . . . Marched one mile west of Weston.

May 4 . . . Still at the same place.

May 5 . . . No move yet.

May 6 . . . Started this morning at 7 o'clock. Marched in the direction of Jacksonville, on the Kanawha and Fairmont pike. The roads are in the worst order of any I have ever seen. Today we marched only about 6 miles.

May 7 . . . Marched today about 3 miles. The artillery and baggage trains can only move from 3 to 5 miles a day, and the infantry has to move accordingly. We have no idea of our destination or whereabouts.

May 11 . . . Been marching every day since the 7th. We are now encamped on Birch River about 15 miles from Summersville. The enemy are reported to hold the place in considerable force. The Regt. undergoes the fatigue of marching splendidly. Today I was much pleased by getting into a canoe to ride across the river—though the other boys had to wade —but about the middle of the river the canoe upset, and as a matter of course I got very wet. We camped in a few hundreds yards of the river, and I am now dry,—but hungry.

May 19 . . . Now encamped near Falling Springs in Greenbrier Co. Va. On the 14th the army left Summersville, and all the time from then until now, has been occupied in marching across the mountains to this place. This is a most beautiful country. We arrived at this place on yesterday evening, and today we are resting. The sun smiles blandly upon the green hills, the cattle are standing in the cool shade of the different groves, and the far off mountains are clothed in a smoky purple hue. What a still, quiet day! Scarcely a sound can be heard to break upon the deep quietude. After so many long and weary marches, one day of rest is very gratefully received, and I have been asleep nearly all day under a low spreading Cedar. I feel much refreshed. One can almost forget, in viewing this peaceful and romantic scenery that a cruel and bloody war is spread broadcast over the land, and sapping the very honey-dew of its existence. Peace (or rather solitude) will surely come sometime, but what will it avail when the vital energies of the people are gone. Can peace restore to home and kindred those manly and heroic soldiers whose bones now bleach upon a thousand battle plains? Long, very long, is the list of broken hearts, cheerless homes already, and what is life, when everything that renders it happy is forever gone? But enough of this now, for no human pen or human power can portray the awful suffering, pain and anxiety of such a war as this. Our favorite, General Jackson was killed at the celebrated battle of the 5th at Fredericksburg. (Note: Gen. Stonewall Jackson was injured May 2 near Chancellorsville. Died May 10, 1863.) Also Gens. Van Dorn and Bragg at Murfreesboro, Tenn.

May 20, '63 . . . Started this morning at an early hour and marched to Greenbrier River beyond Lewisburg. Very hot marching.

May 21 . . . Marched today 4 miles east of White Sulphur Springs.

May 22 . . . Marched 18 miles today in the direction of the Warm Springs in Bath Co. Bad marching on account of the dust. Very tired tonight.

May 23 . . . Marched to the Hot Springs today.

May 24 . . . Shoes have entirely worn out. Got permission to remain in the rear. Commenced raining this evening, and I with 3 other "poor soldiers" put up at a barn.

May 25 . . . Got to ride about 3 miles on our Major's horse. Camped about 8 miles from the Staunton and Parkersburg pike.

May 26 . . . Marched today to the eastern base of Buffalo Mountain. Very tired. Got a letter from Emma today dated May 18.

June 2 . . . Orders came yesterday to leave here today at 10 o'clock, with 4 days' rations of cooked provisions. We have been encamped here ever since the 26th of May. Nothing of interest occurred while here. We do not know where we are going. Many think we are bound again for down the Valley, and then, end our wanderings in a grave on the Rappahannock. It is useless to express an opinion of that cursed clime.

June 3 . . . Our worst fears have been more than realized. We are now encamped on the same ground we occupied when we left Fredericksburg. Why did we come here? Surely there is no Providence that is concerned with the united wish of any people. Fortune has forsaken us, and Fate has thus decreed our gloomy destiny. Although we have been here but an hour or two, everything looks as old and familiar as if we had never left. There is no boundary to one's vision here. And now far, far away northward, may be seen the tents of thousands of that hated race on whose account we have been called to this infernal region. We will leave soon, as the troops around here are ordered to leave tomorrow.

June 4 . . . How beautiful the day! Nature smiles in her luxuriance, full of life and animation, and nothing appears to be unhappy but man himself.

June 5 . . . Left camp last night at 12. We marched about 16 miles in a western direction.

June 6 . . . 9 A.M. We are still at the same place at which we stopped yesterday evening. We have orders to cook 2 days' rations of bread immediately. Several shots of artillery have been heard in the direction of Fredericksburg. A battle is surely imminent. I have some misgivings as to my surviving it. I hope I may.

June 7 . . . We had no fight. On the 6th we marched to the Plank Road. Today we marched to the Orange and Alexandria R.R.—distance about 20 miles.

June 9 . . . Now encamped about 3 miles north of Culpeper Court House,—or as we may more properly say, formed a line of battle here. We came to this place this evening after marching through Culpeper yesterday and in a western direction for about 2 1/2 miles. Our cavalry had a considerable fight with the enemy about one mile from here this morning. The enemy was repulsed. I expect tomorrow will tell a bad tale, for surely it can not be long before it will come. I expect it will be a hard one too. Goodbye for tonight.

June 10 . . . Marched back through Culpeper and about 5 or 6 miles on the road to the Valley.

June 11 . . . Started this morning at 4 1/2 o'clock. Marched about 22 miles and encamped at 4 o'clock in the evening. We are now on the Front Royal road. Very tired indeed.

June 18, 1863 . . . We are now encamped within about 4 miles of Shepherdstown. Since the 11th we had a two-day fight at Winchester. It was a very noisy battle, but not very many were killed. History will detail the plans of the attack, and therefore it is useless for me. The 31st Regt. lost only some two or three men. I got out safely, as I hope to do again in the one that is now pending. I expect we are going into Maryland.

June 21 . . . Still at the same camp. No move

yet, but are expecting orders to do so all the time. I was on guard last night.

June 25 . . . Now encamped 9 miles east of Chambersburg, Pa.

June 29 . . . For the last few days we have been bearing Northward. Nothing of interest transpired during our coming. We are now encamped at Little York, 22 miles east of Harrisburg. No one has any idea where we will go. Our marches have been quite long and severe. The days now are very long and hot. Beautiful June! How I love to look over those green fields and upon the clear blue sky.

June 30 . . . Left York this morning at daylight, and passed over the same road for 20 miles that we traveled in going to that city. Vast amounts of commissary stores of every description were captured at York. Gen. Early made a requisition on the Mayor of the city for $100,000 in money. It was immediately paid, and much of it was afterward expended in payment for horses.

July 1, 1863 . . . Had a fight today at Gettysburg.

July 2 . . . Still in line of battle this morning.

Evening . . . 4 o'clock. The fight is now raging furiously. Awful artillery firing. We are not now engaged. I can not form an idea why we are not, for we have always heretofore been *honored* with going into every fight. We may yet get an opportunity. I hope I may be able to continue my diary hereafter.

July 3 . . . Evening . . . This morning we went into battle. It was a very trying place, as the grape shot and minie balls came to us at right angles. We had not remained in this line very long till I, with many others, was wounded. I was struck on the side of the knee. We are now lying under a tree at a temporary hospital.

July 5 . . . Though yesterday was the Fourth of July it was not spent very pleasantly by me. Yesterday morning all the wounded that could walk had to follow the wagon train. We toiled on all day—suffering considerably. A short time before night my shoes gave out, and had to go it barefoot. When night came, four of us stopped at a straw pile on the side of the road. About 2 o'clock in the morning the enemy's cavalry came sweeping along the road with the wagons—shooting, yelling, and creating the greatest confusion. We heard the noise, and got up and ran back to the woods off the road. This morning we came down to a house, and are now waiting on the porch for breakfast. We are going to try the road again this morning. . . . NOON. . . . Taken prisoner! Sure, and it happened before I got breakfast. Today we marched to the top of Blue Ridge, immediately east of Boonsboro, Md. We were nearly exhausted. Our captors have treated us with the greatest respect. They were greatly discommoded to make us easy and comfortable.

July 6 . . . We marched today to Frederick City, Md. All the boys that were wounded were taken to hospitals and furnished the cleanest kind of clothes and beds. There are a good many "Secesh" ladies in this city.

July 7 . . . Today we got on board a train and arrived at Baltimore on the 8th at 6 A.M.

July 8 . . . We marched down to Fort McHenry about noon and have been standing around in the mud until tonight. Waiting to see where we are to be sent. We have been treated meanly as far as eating anything is concerned. I do not know what is going to become of us or where we are to go. Some think we will not be exchanged at all.

July 9 . . . We are now on board the steam tug Massachusetts. We got on board about 11 o'clock. I think we are bound for Fort Delaware. Some think we will soon be paroled and sent South although many think there is no hope for it very soon. We are crowded so closely in the hold of this vessel that we can not all sit down. We can not see land in any direction, as I was out on deck for some water a few minutes ago. It is most awful warm in here. I hope we may soon get out of it. A little incident occurred today which fully illustrates the meanness of the Yankee race. A young Baltimorian was taken prisoner with us, and when we arrived at Fort McHenry his sister came to see him. She was not allowed even to speak to him, although she could have caught hold of him by reaching out her hand. We were standing outside of the fort with a guard around us, and the brother and sister stood there looking at each other for a few minutes until separated by the guard.

July 10 . . . Arrived at Fort Delaware today at 11 o'clock in the morning. I never passed such a night as I did last night. There were 400 prisoners on board the vessel, and they were so crowded that all could not sit down. The room was very close, and many of the boys were wounded. The bad breath, together with the bad smell of the wounds almost choked us. We appealed to the Officer in charge of us to allow us to go on deck, but he was inexorable, although many of the boys fainted. We are now stowed away in the barracks of the fort, but it is a nice place in comparison with the places in which we have been.

July 11 . . . This is the Sabbath. The time passes away very slowly here. Nothing to change the dull monotony of a pent up life. We all entertain hope of being soon sent south.

July 12 . . . No change in affairs yet. Wrote a letter to Emma today.

July 13 . . . All quiet.

July 14 . . . Nothing new today, only I am nearer starved to death than usual. We only get 6 small crackers and 3 ozs. of meat per day. I am hungry all the time—real hungry. I could eat raw beef now.

July 15 . . . Another day is almost gone. Oh, how I am wasting my precious time. I will surely regret its ever unavoidable waste. We have about come to the conclusion to die here, as there appears to be no hope of being sent away very soon.

July 16 . . . I went out this morning and ate $5 worth of bread and butter!

July 17 . . . I saw some citizen prisoners today that had been arrested for what cause they knew not, and sent to this place. All are from north western Virginia, and some from my own county.

July 18 . . . Nothing new today.

July 19 . . . This is the Sabbath, but darn such a place as this is. It isn't fit for a Sunday to come here.

July 20 . . . All quiet along the lines today. I am most infernal hungry. It is now two o'clock and I haven't had anything to eat but three crackers and meat enough for one bite.

July 21 . . . The same old thing over today. We can't hear anything from the outside world at all. The guards tell us that Vicksburg has surely fallen, and are quite jubilant over it. We don't believe it. They tell us that our Confederacy is nearly conquered and subjugated. But so long as there are a thousand men together in the Southern states who can lift a gun or crawl through a cane brake, they will never cease to fight the invader of this country! *Unconsciously,* the Southern people are truly warlike, and far more capable of carrying on a war than their enemies suppose.

July 22 . . . All quiet.

July 23 . . . The same old thing over.

July 26 . . . Sunday. Nothing new.

July 27 . . . Have the headache today.

July 29 . . . Heavy rain last night.

July 30 . . . Received a letter from Mr. Crim yesterday evening containing some of the "one thing needful", and the night of the 28th some villain stole my pictures. Today I received a letter from Emma.

July 31 . . . Nothing new today.

Aug. 4 . . . There has been so little transpiring the last few days that I did not care about keeping my diary. One or two prisoners have been shot by the sentries during the past few days, for disobedience of orders.

Aug. 11 . . . New Barracks are being erected here, although there are enough now to accommodate 10,000 prisoners. To look at the general aspect of affairs, it is my opinion that we boys are at *Fort Delaware.* All the "Greenbacks" that I rec. from home have played out, and now I have to go it like the rest. I have not heard from home but once.

Aug. 13 . . . Today I received a letter from Julia. They had not received any of my last letters and were therefore anxious about me. This is a "Party Remembrance" day, as in 1860 everyone comprising the party made a promise to remember that day every following year. In 1861 I was on Allegheny Mountain. In 1862 I was in Lynchburg. In 1863 in Fort Delaware.

Aug. 16 . . . Sunday. Another hot day has gone. "One calm day is added now to quiet age, and one happy day to hopeful youth." I received a letter today from Mrs. Allie J. Crim, my sister.

Aug. 17 . . . There was a bad storm in these parts last night. We thought this land was going to be subjugated in the lake. There was some tall cursing going on in the meantime.

Aug. 20 . . . The prisoners were all separated today according to their respective states.

Aug. 21 . . . Nothing new, only I am nearly starved to death. Got a letter from home today —from Julia,—together with some greenbacks.

Aug. 22 . . . Nothing new today.

Aug. 23 . . . Received a letter from Jasper.

Aug. 26 . . . Last night was as cold as the devil and the weather is quite wintry this A.M.

Aug. 31 . . . This morning is more wintry than any we have had yet, but we drew blankets from the Yankees. A rebel was killed last night by a guard. He was killed foolishly, but I expect the fellow is better off, at least he can not be much worse off.

Sept. 1 . . . Received a letter today from Emma, also a Greenback enclosed.

Sept. 8 . . . Got a letter from Al Crim today. Also one from Em and J.T.L. Em's and Al's had some of the one thing needful here.

Sept. 10 . . . Last night was cool. There is some talk of being sent away soon.

Sept. 13 . . . Nothing new, except I have got the mumps!

Sept. 18 . . . Nothing transpired here to write about.

Sept. 21 . . . Monday. A beautiful day. Some Rebs left here on the 19th. Some think all of us will leave soon.

Sept. 24 . . . Received a letter today from J. T. Latham and also one from Julia. Very glad to hear for "you all". No change of affairs yet.

Oct. 2 . . . Received a letter from Em a few days ago, which said a box of provender, etc. was shipped to me on the 22nd of Sept., but the thing hasn't got here yet, although I am anxiously awaiting its coming.

Oct. 5 ... Three months ago today the Yankees caught me. Damn that day.

Oct. 7 ... Got the box from home today.

Oct. 11 ... Sunday. A long, quiet, beautiful and *dreary* day. It appears as if evening will never come. A long, listless, hazy October Sunday. Nothing under heaven to make the time pass pleasantly. I read a novel—"John Halifax"—today, but it was so short it did not suffice. Again, rumors of leaving soon. If it is only true!

Oct. 13 ... Got 2 letters from home yesterday, one of which contained some of "the one thing needful". Cold weather now, and I have got a very bad cold.

Oct. 25 ... We left Fort Delaware this morning in the steamer "Ashland" for Point Lookout.

Oct. 26 ... Arrived at the Point this evening, but have to remain on the vessel until morning. We are so closely crowded that it is impossible for all to sit down.

Oct. 27, 1863 ... Left the boat this morning, and were sent to the prisoner's camp. We were divided off into companies and divisions. Mine is Company E, 7th Division.

Nov. 1 ... This is Sunday. A very clear and bright day, and the air very sharp. The bay is covered with large white-crested waves.

Nov. 2 ... Received a letter from Jim today.

$1 enclosed. Put a brick fireplace to our "house" today.

Nov. 4 . . . Got a letter from the "old lady" today—wanting me to write to her *"dater"*.

Nov. 16 . . . Blue Monday. Nothing new. The history of one day is the history of all.

Nov. 17 . . . Went out of camp today for some wood. The first time I have been out of the *ring*. Nothing new.

Nov. 18 . . . Quite unwell today.

Nov. 19 . . . No better. Have a dismal hurting under my *apron*.

Nov. 20 . . . Some better today. Haven't got a letter from home in reply to any I have written on the Point yet.

Nov. 21 . . . Got worse today. Suffering considerably.

Nov. 22 . . . My belly hurts awful.

Nov. 23 . . . No change yet in *internal* affairs.

Nov. 24 . . . Some little better this morning. A dreary, dark day. Been drizzling rain all last night and today.

Nov. 25 . . . Left Fort Delaware this day one month ago.

Nov. 26 . . . Quite unwell. A very beautiful day. No letter from home yet.

Nov. 27 . . . My birthday! I am just 22 years old tonight. I wonder where I will be my next anniversary? My disease has not abated much yet. Have to use laudanum, etc.

Nov. 28 ... Commenced to rain early this morning. What can I do to make the time pass quickly? Only sit and watch the boys tramping around in the mud and rain. Nothing to read, and nothing that a man can eat. The crackers are as hard as flint stone, and full of worms. I don't believe God ever intended for one man to pen another up and keep him in this manner. We ought to have enough to eat, anyhow.— "Dam Old Abe and old Jeff Davis, Dam the day I 'listed"—

Nov. 29 ... Cold as the devil this morning. A freezing sleety rain.

Nov. 30 ... Still about, but nearly frozen to death.

Dec. 1 ... Got a box of provender from home today. Was appointed clerk for the Div. Surgeon this morning.

Dec. 2 ... Got 2 letters from home with "munish" in them. *Mr. Clerk* is going to have a tent to himself shortly.

Dec. 3 ... Nothing new today.

Dec. 4 ... Very quiet today.

Dec. 5 ... A pleasant day. Some very heavy artillery firing heard in the west. No news.

Dec. 6 ... Moving tents today and fixing up as though it were the intention to remain here for some time to come. A heavy frost last night.

Dec. 7 ... No news for this line.

Dec. 11 . . . Nothing interesting has transpired for the last few days. I am now in a tent to myself. Dine with the M.D.'s, etc.

Dec. 12 . . . A very pleasant day.

Dec. 13 . . . Had a storm last night and plenty of rain this morning. On this day 2 years ago the battle of Allegheny was fought. Last year, the first battle of Fredericksburg.

Dec. 16 . . . "All quiet along the lines tonight". The Provost Marshal shot 4 prisoners today, while he was drunk, but fortunately did not kill any. One had his leg amputated, and another his arm.

Dec. 19 . . . Some talk of our exchange, but there is little confidence placed in it.

Dec. 20 . . . Nearly frozen to death. Have to roll up in my blanket and keep dancing about to keep from giving up. Some Rebs going to leave tomorrow Prov. says.

Dec. 24 . . . Christmas Eve! Dam such a place for Christmas to come. Tonight is the most beautiful night I ever saw. The Rebs who left here a day or two ago we think went to City Point.

Dec. 25 . . . Christmas. A very quiet day. Been reading a novel all day. Not much sign of Christmas here.

Dec. 28 . . . Been raining all night and continuing today. Some more Rebs to leave again so I have heard.

Dec. 30 . . . No Rebs left since the first load.

Dec. 31 . . . New Year's Eve . . . A perfect gale has been blowing over the Point all day, and it has not ceased raining or storming yet. The Bay looks awful. The old year has about gone . . . "Its mark is on each brow, its shadow in each heart. In its swift course it passed over the battle field, where the gathered strength of hosts was striven, and the grass, green from the field of carnage waves above the crushed and mouldering skeleton. It came like a wreath of mist at eve, but ere it faded into viewless air, it heralded its millions to their long home in the dim land of dreams. Remorseless Time! —Spirit of unsleeping power! What powers can stay thee in thy silent course, or melt thy iron heart to pity?"

1864

Jan. 1, 1864 . . . A beautiful day.

Jan. 2 . . . An extremely cold night and very much after the same fashion this evening.

Jan. 5 . . . Warm and foggy. No news afloat.

Jan. 8 . . . The first snow I have seen this winter, fell today. A sizeable amount.

Jan. 9 . . . A very cold day.

Jan. 14 . . . The Yanks gave me a suit of clothes today. Clever, sure.

Jan. 15 . . . Received a letter from Miss Cora N. Crim. Nice warm weather now.

Feb. 2 . . . Ground Hog day. Saw his shadow.

Feb. 8 . . . Received a letter today from J. T. Latham. Have not heard from home for a long time.

Feb. 14 . . . Had inspection of camp today. Two light canoes were found, with which some of the prisoners were probably going to make their escape, but failed. Nothing new has transpired in our lives here. The events of one day are so like all others that it is difficult to distinguish one from another.

Feb. 16 . . . A light snow last night, and today is very cold and windy. No letters yet.

Feb. 19 . . . Last night was the coldest of any night this winter. Some of the prisoners have only one blanket, and have to lie on the ground. Last night I could hear them dancing and running about all night to keep from freezing. The sick have a hard time, no proper diet or medical treatment. Haven't had a letter from home for 2 weeks.

Feb. 22 . . . A warm beautiful day. A few big rain drops are falling. This is a Yankee National day. They gave us plenty of whiskey, punch, etc. but I, being very abstemious, did not imbibe. Have received no letters from home for nearly 3 weeks, but got one today from Uncle Thomas of Ill. A negro Regt. came on the Point today.

Feb. 25 . . . Wonder of wonders! We folks, American citizens and white men, have negroes on post guarding us. When they first made their appearance, a prisoner laughed at the awkwardness of one of the negroes, when an officer drew his revolver and snapped twice at him, and then, cut him dangerously over the hand with his saber. All this was done for laughing at a negro! Evening: Received one letter from home and one from Mr. Latham.

Feb. 26 . . . Negro patrol out on guard last night. Shot at someone . . . (illegible) several prisoners . . .

Feb. 27 . . . All quiet today.

Feb. 29 . . . A dark, gloomy day.

March 1 . . . Continues very foggy. Some talk of part of the prisoners leaving for the South soon.

March 5 . . . Received two letters from home; one from Ma. Isn't it strange,—the first letter I ever received from my mother; but writing to one at home is writing to all, and my receiving one is hearing from all.

March 6 . . . Sunday night. Cold, cheerless and gloomy. No fire, and have to go to bed to keep warm. Some little hope of going South has again cast a glorious light in our gloomy hearts.

March 7 . . . A clear, cold day. Tired of living. I am sorry I ever came into this mean world, but more sorry I was born in this cursed land.

March 8 . . . Been raining nearly all day. There is no hope of ever getting out of this hell-hole.

March 9 . . . Received a letter from "little sister" today, with a twig of cedar.

March 10 . . . A dismal day. Cold and rainy. Several of my friends started to Dixie land yesterday, among whom is the Surgeon of this Division. They are of the peculiarly fortunate class. I have thought no man would be willing to die if left to himself, but now I can truly say—"There is a future, O thank God." This cold, cruel world! Why is man born in it to live nothing but a life pregnant with blasted hopes and complete misery? "A glass to the dead already—Hurrah for the next that dies".

March 12 . . . Another beautiful day. Received a letter from the "young Esq." today. Sickness has increased very rapidly during the last two days. I am thinking "Mr. Pneumonia" and Messrs "Fever and Dysentery" will have a jolly time this spring among the poor Rebs.

March 13 . . . Nothing transpired today, only some prisoners who have taken the oath of Parole for the war, left the prison—gone to someplace, God only knows where.

March 14 . . . Rec. a letter from Miss Campbell to her brother, who's sick in the hospital. Evening: Heard some doleful news for us: "No more exchanging of prisoners unless the South agrees to exchange regardless of Color", which will never be done.

Mar. 15 . . . Poor Jim Campbell died today. He was sick a long time. I wrote to his friends today.

March 16 . . . A cold clear day. Some more prisoners were ordered to be ready to leave today. It was a great surprise after what was in the paper.

March 17 . . . A load of prisoners left today. Rec. a letter from Allie.

March 18 . . . No news of any kind. The

negroes on guard last night kept up a mighty fuss.

March 20 . . . Easter Sunday. No eggs or anything good.

March 21 . . . A very cold day. Another vessel has arrived, which is some sign of a few more prisoners leaving soon.

March 22 . . . A dismal day. One of the nastiest storms I ever saw is going on now. The Bay looks terrible. The waves look as though they would submerge the Point. It is very cold, and none of the prisoners have wood. Dismal times.

March 23 . . . Last night was the roughest of any we have had here. The snow has drifted to the depth of several feet. The after part of the day was genial and warmer.

March 24 . . . No news—not even a rumor of any kind.

March 25 . . . A very nice morning, but the night came with heavy clouds and torrents of rain. Received a letter from Julee, containing $1. I wrote to her this evening.

March 26 . . . No news. Have been quite unwell today, bad cold and cough.

March 27 . . . Sunday. Still unwell.

March 28 . . . Received letter from Allie today, also one from Miss C. and one from Uncle Tom. A beautiful day. Warm and genial.

March 29 . . . A cold windy day. The Bay

looks awful. Feel very much under the weather this morning.

March 30 . . . The weather continues cold.

March 31 . . . Cold and damp but beautiful sunshine this evening.

April 1 . . . A beautiful day. Had to move my tent, as there seems to be a general revision of the Camp. Mine is a nice tent. I will furnish it hereafter.

April 2 . . . Another rainy day. The place where I moved my tent was very soft, and the rain made it nothing but a pile of mud. The water and mud is about four feet deep inside, and the heavy gale from the North has raised the stakes of the frame on which the tent is placed, out of the ground. It is bound to be demolished. Our chimney too is melting away. A word now about our houses and chimneys in camp. About half of the camp is of large Sibley tents, the remainder of common "A" tents. The former have from 15-20 inmates, the latter from 4-6. I, with a young man from Halifax occupy an "A" tent, which is the Call tent of the Division. Many of the smaller tents are placed on wooden frames about 2 feet high—made out of cracker boxes. A large bunk is made with joints so it can be folded up in the morning. Some have houses made altogether of cracker boxes, and are large and commodious—bearing different names, as "Eldon Hall", "In for the War", "2.40", "Crescent Hall", etc. Chimneys are built of bricks which were made without being burnt. They last well, if allowed to stand for a few days without being rained upon.

April 3 . . . Slept at the Surgeon's tent last night. Quite cold today. I don't know what to do with myself,—have a notion to sell out.

April 5 . . . Yesterday we fixed up our tent in gay style. Stole enough planks to make a good floor and other necessaries. The rain has not ceased for 48 hours and is still coming. Many of the tents are a foot deep in water. No wood for fires, and the air very cold. Hard times.

April 6 . . . A tolerably nice day, quite cool, but no rain!

April 9 . . . Pleasant weather from the 6th to this time, but today we have more rain.

April 10 . . . A beautiful morn but an ugly eve. No news today. Two boys wore barrel shirts for the crime of stealing today.

April 11 . . . Have nothing to write today, only there is a rumor of more prisoners going to leave today or tomorrow.

April 12 . . . A perfect spring day. So warm and mild. Got a big snort of whiskey yesterday —felt powerfully rich and independent for a short time, but the affair wound up with a nasty headache.

April 14 . . . Took some physic today, and feel some better this evening. The Yankees inspected the prison camp today. Some of the prisoners left yesterday on a limited parole. Another Regt. of negroes came to the Point to guard us. It is the 4th Regt. of Maryland Colored U.S. Troops.

April 15 . . . Quite well now. Received a letter from Allie today. Rumor of exchanges has played out. Rained a little bit tonight.

April 17 . . . A regular spring day. Sunday. An occasional shower with dark heavy clouds.

April 18 . . . Another day is gone, and a most beautiful one too, but a little cool this evening.

April 19 . . . A fresh rumor afloat now, of more prisoners leaving soon. Got the blues this evening. Gloomy times, surely.

April 21 . . . Received a letter from Hon. M. G. Brown today.

April 22 . . . Recd. 2 letters from home today, one from Ma and one from Julee. Each contained some of "the needful."

April 24 . . . Received another letter from home today, containing $5. It also said my release from prison would soon come, through the influence of Mr. Brown. Said it is already accomplished.

April 27 . . . Some prisoners left today for the South. Only a small number here, and all of those are sick or have lost a limb. My tent was moved yesterday, and I am now living in the Surgeon's tent at the hospital. The night is far spent. Tattoo has long since died out, excepting the notes of a distant bugle. I feel quite sad tonight. These evil times in which I am peculiarly situated have fully developed themselves tonight. I can't write more, for that old bugle is full of melancholy sadness and loneliness.

April 28 . . . "O time, fleet, fleet away. Oh linger not in this drear apathetic strain. Make fortune to elevate, or crush wholly underneath. Haste thee, time, and haste thee on."

April 30 . . . Night. Why is it that I am always unhappy? A sad gloom almost continually pervades my inmost soul. I can not tell why it is or from whence it comes.

May 3 . . . We were much surprised this morning by an order for more prisoners to go South. Only about 300 went, and all of those mostly non-combatants.

May 6 . . . Today the Provost Marshal sent for me to report to his office immediately. I went, but the Provost had gone out of Camp this morning, leaving an order for me to report at 3 o'clock, when he expected to be back. I did not see him, and do not know what he wanted with me.

May 8 . . . Sunday. A very hot day. Haven't

heard anything about what the Provost Marshal wished with me. Quite anxious now about news from our army in Virginia.

May 9 . . . Was called out today to visit the post Commander in reference to my parole. It amounted to nothing more than for me to take the Oath of Allegiance, which I could not do of course.

May 11 . . . Night. A very hot day, but tonight a heavy thunder storm is progressing. Glorious news from our army in Northern Virginia. If it is only true! Haven't received a letter from home for several days. I expect they are looking for me home—a disappointment to them.

May 13 . . . A damp day, heavy thunder showers passing all day. Exciting news from our army in Virginia.

May 17 . . . Morning. Several hundred Reb prisoners arrived here last night from General Lee's army. They report dismal work in Va. They are all confident of our ultimate success in this battle. Evening: Saw some prisoners from the Regt. to which I belong. Nothing new.

May 18 . . . More prisoners came in today, but none from the command to which I belong.

May 19 . . . Found a member of my company —E. T. Corder, among the new prisoners. He gives a very graphic description of the recent awful battle.

May 20 . . . Nothing of interest has occurred today.

May 25 . . . More prisoners from Gen. Lee's army have come here during the last few days. We think from reports, our army must be successful.

May 26 . . . Rec. a letter from Baltimore, which said the clothing I wrote for a few days since was shipped to me.

May 29 . . . It is quite lovely today. Sunday. The sun shines brightly and the deep azure blue of heaven is unsurpassingly beautiful, but it cannot dispel the melancholy which shrouds my soul. Oh sad the hour which gave me being! Why do men seek for happiness in this world, when all who lived before never found it? or why was man created? Here's the ever present answer: "This state of being is but preparatory to, or the vestibule of a better state hereafter". I believe it. Then why not do better? I'll try, —I do, but this eternal sadness creeps upon the mind, and I become perfectly careless of the present, and still more so of the future. "Stop this gab!" Here I'm in a Yankee prison, with but little hope of getting out, and none whatever of surviving the war. Let me firmly look fate in the face and boldly strive to accomplish that which duty says perform.

May 30 . . . Received the package of clothing today—everything came nicely, and suits me well.

June 5 . . . Sunday. Have a nice floor in my house now. Received a letter from Allie yesterday—some talk of a box of provender being sent to me. Rations of coffee are now withdrawn from the prisoners. Smack out of money now.

June 7 . . . A clear, beautiful day. I've been looking at the green branches of a tall maple tree whose top towers above the parapet of the prison. How gracefully its branches wave in the soft breezes from off the Bay. How pure, how beautiful. It is surely emblematical of purity and also partakes of the innocent. A lady rode in to camp yesterday! The only one I have seen for many months. But I haven't *spoken* to anything of the kind for more than a year!

June 9 . . . More prisoners came into camp today, and one was a woman disguised as a Confederate soldier. She says she has been in a Co. of Artillery from her native county, with her brother, ever since the war began. She was driver. The Yankee officials credit her report and think she is purely virtuous.

June 10 . . . A heavy rain last night. It doesn't rain here, either, but pours in unbroken volume.

June 11 . . . Morning. Four large transports are anchored off the Point. We hope they have come to take us away, although we don't know anything about it. Will find out today. Wrote a letter to Julee yesterday.

June 12 . . . Those transports did not come for us. One brought more Rebs to prison, and the others, for some Yankee wounded who were here. No news of any kind today. Our *little woman* is still in camp, but wishes much to be sent away.

June 13 . . . Received a letter today from Julee with $2 in it. It was very opportune, for I was clean broke. My chum is now gone for a letter from his home, with more of the "needful" in it. We are going to live well, sure. I don't like a thing very well that I was told today: the disease I have had but slightly all winter and spring, has now assumed a chronic form, and is of course cured with difficulty. I'm not a bit afraid of it, for if I keep as well as I am now, I will live a long time anyway. There is big talk of there never being an exchange. We are resigned to our fate. But God knows it is very hard.

June 14 . . . Another day is gone. Calm, beautiful and glorious. Oh how beautiful nature must appear in the country now! It seems strange I should live here. I want my time to pass rapidly for it is nothing but a blank in my existence. I have learned much however, in better things. In fact it is a good place for meditation.

June 21 . . . Nothing of interest has transpired since the 14th. A few more prisoners have come in—two from the Regt. to which I belong. All of the money of my last remittance is gone, but am now looking for more. . . . Various rumors from Richmond are afloat now. Some say Gen. Grant has been wholly defeated, while others say, nothing but awful fighting has taken place yet.

June 29 . . . Have seen no letter from home since the 21st and have heard no news but the never ending camp rumors. There has been no rain for 2 weeks, and the ground is covered with dust. The air has been quite cool for 2 days past, but before, it was excessively hot. If we can form an opinion from rumors and Yankee papers, there have been some wicked times of late in Virginia. But all by which we are governed is the quotation of the gold market. At the beginning of this campaign, gold was only worth 1.72 per cent, but now only 2.36 per cent, which shows clearly their Public affairs are not prospering well.

June 30 . . . Received 2 letters from home today—one from Julee and one from Emma, both of which had "munish" in them. I can't write anything I wish in one page of note paper, which will occasion my trying very hard to send them a *blockade* letter, which will give them the exact "position" here.

July 4 . . . All quite still today. Two gunboats lying close to the Point have exhibited an unusual number of national flags, as this is their national day. Have heard no salutes yet.

July 8 . . . Gold has been quoted the last few days at from 2.50 to 2.90 per centum. Heard of the sinking of the C. S. Sloop Alabama by a U.S. Gunboat off the coast of France. We did not credit the report until it seemed credited in the papers. Very dry now. Nothing but dust, dust! No papers were allowed in camp this morning. We think something has gone wrong with the Yanks,—at least they would not object to our seeing any news favorable to themselves. Heavy clouds indicate a coming storm.

July 9, 1864 . . . This is Saturday night. Elam Corder has gone to bed, and I have been sitting up ruminating. It seems that the stopping of newspapers is a fixed fact, as none came in this morning. My belly still pains much now and then—one reason of it is the want of proper food. The folks at home said they were going to send me a box of provender, but the thing hasn't come yet. I don't mind living on one thing for ten or fifteen months, but I'm out when it comes to two or three years. *Old Mr. Ewell* has intercepted my box of provisions I expect.

July 10 . . . This is Sunday. It has been the

longest day to drag out that I have had here. I thought night would never come. I've just lit my candle, and find a sensible relief in it. I'm nearly starved to death now days,—we get enough sour bread and *salt horse,* but we have lived on it so long, it appears we can hardly eat any more of it. Between being half starved and half sick, together with nothing to read, and no where to go or promenade, we have a hard wearisome time of it. There is nothing green in our camp—nothing but the bare dusty earth, and hot! I never felt heat before.

July 11 . . . Another hot, dusty, sultry day is gone. Towards evening heavy thunder clouds appeared in the South, with every prospect of rain, but they passed without a shower. Some prisoners left yesterday for prison camps in more northern states—New York we think. I am told this camp will be broken up, and all of us taken farther in the interior. Such movements look little like there will be an exchange.

July 14 . . . Considerable excitement now in camp about the "Rebel raid". About a thousand prisoners took the Oath of Allegiance to the U.S. Government today. Poor, deluded fellows hope to better their condition!

July 15 . . . More rumors about the Rebs around Washington City. But as no papers can come in, we can hardly form an opinion. Some of the prisoners who went out to take the Oath yesterday, have been coming back all day in little squads, under the protection of negro guards. It would not be safe to come in alone while they are procuring their blankets, etc. None of the prisoners are allowed to speak to them.

July 16 . . . Moved my tent today. The Yankee Doctor in charge of the camp, gave me a new tent, and I now use the old one as a fly. Sent nine sick men to the hospital today. The sickness appears to be increasing, and the deaths average eight every day. News from Washington is very scarce. Not even a rumor.—Later— Rumors afloat this evening seem confirmed, viz, "A general parole of prisoners to commence on the 24th inst. Capture of a Fort near to, and the shelling of Washington City; defeat of Gen. Sherman, and annihilation of Sheridan's command."

July 17, Sunday . . . A long, long day. I feel so tired that I haven't energy to draw a long breath. The days always linger, but the weeks and months seem to pass more quickly.

July 19 . . . Elam Corder received a box from his friends at home today. It contained a large ham, one large can of honey, and one of butter, with various other little articles. It was very opportune, as we're nearly starved to death on "salt horse" and sourbread. I'm looking for one myself every day. A bad rumor came in camp today. That Gen. J. E. Johnson's army had suffered a severe defeat in the southwest, together with the capture of many prisoners. We hardly credit it.

July 20 . . . The rumors of yesterday evening, have today proved to be false. But a rumor—or rather a Yankee paper says, an exchange is now certainly agreed upon. It may be so, but we have heard that song so often. Received a letter today from Cousin Sena Hall. Elam Corder and I are now living well on ham, etc.

July 22 . . . Scarcely a rumor has been in camp for the last two days. No newspapers have been seen of a later date than the 15th. The sky looks like Indian summer, so hazy and smoky. Haven't received my box of eatables yet, neither any letters from home for nearly an entire month.

July 24 . . . This is Sunday. The sun has not shown itself here today. There appear to be no clouds, only an impenetrable haze. It seems that we will never have any more rain. The Bay is very calm now—not a ripple breaks its glassy smoothness. We can only see a short distance on the water, for the haze seems to blend sky and water. Some prisoners left here today for Elmira, New York. Clothing was given to some of the prisoners today—both do not speak very favorably for our getting away on exchange.

July 26 . . . Had a big rain yesterday morning, and a strong wind, but the earth was so dry that it swallowed it up immediately, and it is as dusty now as ever. A rumor in camp this evening that Gen. Johnston's army in Ga. attacked Gen. Sherman, and defeated him after two days hard fighting.

July 27 . . . "Evening's somber shadows have again cast their long length" across our Prison Camp. The day has passed away as hundreds of others have gone, without leaving a trace by which it can be distinguished from the blended record of the past. No news, no letters, no box, no nothing today. Rumors have been very quiet. How lonesome it is. What a cussed way of spending the short time we have to live. "Evil stars" are now certainly in the ascendancy.

July 28 . . . Time still glides imperceptibly away. But it is leaving its mark, however obscure it may now appear. The reported defeat of Gen. Sherman now seems confirmed, i.e. by the outside reports.

July 29 . . . More prisoners were sent away today. We don't know where they are going.

Aug. 1 . . . Today I had two letters from home, and both of them had money, but I have not received it yet. The Provost Marshal does not allow any money in camp. It must be either checks or orders on the Sutler for the amount specified in the letter. News from the different armies is quite vague and contradictory. But it is certainly favorable for the Rebs if we may form an opinion.

Aug. 5 . . . News from Gen. Grant is quite cheering to us. There are big tales in the papers about Gen. Lee opening hundreds of pieces of artillery on Gen. Grant's massed columns, and the consequent losses, etc. etc. I am thinking big events are transpiring out doors, too!

Aug. 6 . . . A very heavy thunder storm about daylight. There was a waterspout on the Bay, and it was plainly visible from our camp. It was surely a curiosity. This evening another big storm is coming up, as we can see the *baldheaded* clouds, and can hear the heaviest artillery. El Corder's box has about played out now, and I'm real hungry tonight. I wish the folks would send a bite to me now and then.

Aug. 7 . . . Another long, long Sunday has almost gone. Now and then a day will come that seems to pass real quickly, but most of them drag wearily, very wearily out. Oh, my God, will I ever get out of this hell hole? Just think! I haven't seen a green field, a shrub or tree, and not even a running brook for more than a year! I don't believe in the right of one man to pen another up and keep him at this rate.

Aug. 8 . . . A negro sentinel shot and killed

a prisoner last night. It was very uncalled for, and amounts to nothing but a clear murder. Very little news of any kind reaches us now. I got a pair of new shoes and an undergarment from the Yanks yesterday by using a little strategy. Had a fine mess of watermelons today.

Aug. 9 . . . Received two letters today, one from Jap and one from HER. I dropped a note to *one* of them today.

Aug. 10 . . . News is powerfully dull now days. A big thunder storm is coming up now. Must walk out and see its sublime beauty.

Aug. 13 . . . Four years ago on this day a "Pleasure Party" promised to remember it afterwards every year. On that day a party of young ladies and gentlemen took a walk to a very picturesque part of the mountains near my native village. We left our names on a card secreted in a dry part of a ledge, and would for every year note the changes that should come upon us all. "Some are scattered now and fled. Some are married, some are dead". Death has early overtaken three or four of those assembled there, and I now find myself in a Yankee prison, after three years of strange adventures in a dismal war, but am almost wholly ignorant of what time has done for others of our party, excepting those who have fallen in defense of their country's honor and liberty.

Aug. 14 . . . Received the money due me

from several letters which came a long time ago—$4. There is another prisoner in camp by my name, and I got in addition to mine, three dollars of his. I gave him his money.

Aug. 15 . . . All prisoners brought to this place in the months of July, August and Sept. 1863, have to leave here tomorrow. "Where are they going?" is on every tongue. I came here on the 27th of October 1863.

Aug. 16 . . . Very little news today, but any amount of rumors about an exchange. Some are very confident that those called out yesterday will be sent South, but others are equally confident the other way. Letters from home are very few and far between now.

Aug. 17 . . . Received a letter from Julee dated the 12th, in which was stated the consoling fact that she had started me a box of provender. I think it will be here soon. Had a very heavy thunder shower this evening. It did not rain, but the water poured down so thick and dense that a fish could have swum anywhere in the air.

Aug. 18 . . . Morning. Had a very curious dream last night. Dreamed of: "My Lady". I don't know of anyone like her, but if I ever see her, I will certainly know her. I thought her a perfect angel, but too beautiful and too angelical for me to address. I woke up desperately smitten, and can hardly drive her out of my mind.

Aug. 19 ... A dark, gloomy day. It reminded me so much of last winter and spring when I heard the rain beating against my tent. The sun has not shown itself at all. I've been dismally restless all day, and there has been nothing to enliven the dull hours.

Aug. 20 ... Bully! Got said box from home today. It contained a hog's "half stem", a gal. of applebutter, one can of preserves, one can of butter, dried beef, sugar, tea, coffee, etc. etc. I've no appetite whatever this evening to eat anything. Has been real chilly all day and very dark and lonely. Very little news from Virginia or the South West. A friend proposed to me today to leave this *peaceful, prosperous* country, and link our destinies with the rising greatness of Brazil. The offer is certainly enticing, but I'll wait the present turn of affairs.

Aug. 22 ... I am getting *fat* now days. That Brazilian proposition caused me some deep thought. Oh, if I only knew whether there would be an exchange during the war! Tom Ashcraft made his escape today while on detail. He was hotly pursued a few hours later, but we think he is gone *good*.

Aug. 23 ... Tom was caught and brought in camp this morning. He was pestered with a chain and 24 lb. ball to his leg.

Aug. 25 ... Some more prisoners came in camp today—300. They were captured on the

Weldon R.R. Dismal hot weather now,—had to go clean naked to keep from burning up. The said provender box still affords satisfaction.

Aug. 26 . . . Much scurvy in camp. I'm afraid lots of the Rebs will rot clean away.

Aug. 27 . . . A regular fall day. Can feel a tinge of chilly air this evening.

Aug. 29 . . . A beautiful clear day. The air is hot, but very bracing and buoyant. There are two money letters on the Point for me, but there's no knowing when I will receive them. The idea of taking a Brazilian trip is growing upon me. I'll leave the country if not exchanged.

Sept. 1 . . . A real autumn day. Got a very nasty headache and don't feel well. News is very scarce now days, hardly a rumor. I feel downcast this evening. Oh my God, what a cursed life this is. I don't want to leave the continent, and especially home, but I won't die in here, so help me God, if I can get out on condition of leaving the country. I want old father Time to get along fast, fast, fast. Existing here is worse than not existing at all. It is hell and damnation mingled.

Sept. 6 . . . Received a letter from Julee today. A thunder storm is coming.

Sept. 7 . . . Morning. This is one of the nicest mornings I have seen for a long time. Tolerably cool however. There was no mail yesterday as the storm was too severe for small craft to travel on the waters. News from the front has been scarce, but rumors more numerous than usual.

Sept. 8 . . . Dark milky clouds overspread the sky this afternoon, and a slow drizzling rain has now commenced. Not a breeze even, is stirring. It is a mighty lonesome time. Gods! if I could but foretell future events for a while.

Sept. 9 . . . All prisoners belonging to the C.S. Navy were called out, for what purpose we know not. That poor old box has played out. Not a vestige left of its former glory. Real fall weather now, days and nights quite cool.

Sept. 10 . . . Bad rumors today—am told Atlanta has surely gone up. Got a letter from cousin Mell Hall. Going to write to her tomorrow.

Sept. 12 . . . Received a letter from Allie today.

Sept. 13 . . . A boat load of sick Rebs leave this evening. None but those permanently sick or disabled can go. I am sick myself this evening. Got a hellish bad cold.

Sept. 16 . . . Ate a fine mess of crabs last night. No news of any sort these times—haven't seen a paper for weeks. Letters from home are scarce now days. The Yanks took a few more Rebs out of camp today to finish up the load.

They were all sick and disabled. It is a curious sight in camp when a boat load is being made up. The sick and wounded wishing to be examined, and the *well* ones slyly offering large bribes, or closely watching any shadow of an opening for going.

Sept. 17 . . . Received 3 money letters today. They were advertised 3 weeks ago. Had a royal melon to eat. They are *cheap*—only cost $1!

Sept. 18 . . . Oh what a long day, and Sunday at that. I want old Father Time to travel fast while I'm here. I want him to "git along". We celebrated the Sabbath with another fine watermelon. It was as much as five of us could get around. Quiet times now in this *city*.

Sept. 21 . . . Evening's somber shadows have appeared again. It is the dullest time now ever known here. Even rumors have become scarce.

Sept. 22 . . . A rumor in camp this evening that Gen. Early in the Valley has got a hellish licking. A dreary day—cloudy and lonely.

Sept. 23 . . . What shall I write? O time, speed away. God, how can I stay here longer! I believe I'll become a perfect idiot soon. Perpetual confinement not only impairs the physical powers, but its baneful influence is felt in the inmost soul. Time is passing so rapidly, while in here when I think of its waste. Time passing now is gone forever.

Sept. 27 . . . Thirteen hundred new Rebs

came in camp today. They belong to Gen. Early. It seems that Gen. Early's command was not so badly defeated as was reported. Only 1300 captured, instead of 5000. *He* took 4000 Yanks in out of the wet.

Oct. 9 . . . Since the last date some little change has taken place. Several Rebs from the Regt. to which I belong have come in, one from my own company. Cold as the devil last night.

Oct. 10 . . . Sometimes I think I'll quit my diary altogether. I've almost despaired of late. For what, under heaven, have I to hope? Life is a curse, happiness is a myth anyhow. What have we to live for? Better off in the grave. It is strange that life is a curse, when Man's genius is so infernal. Outside of this hell, bright life flows in every vein, and health is manifest on every rosy cheek. Freedom to do and act, and perform those duties God intended when he animated this vile clay. I'm going to be forgotten and uncared for by all my fellow men, but what thought or care have I for anyone in return? I do not wish sympathy. But— forgotten, did I say? Within the quiet of my far off home, kind parents are now commending to His care their absent son, and sisters too, sigh that I tarry so long. And within me a voice says, For thee, for thee, I only care to live.

Oct. 14 . . . Oh sweet but sad memory! But

how strange that I should be already tired of life, expecting no pleasure in the future, and thinking of happiness as being alone connected with childhood's sunny days — when I am young yet, actually just appearing on the threshold of adult life. It is well. No misfortunes that hereafter may appear upon my life's chequered pathway, will deprive me of happiness or contentment, for none of either exist, nor do I claim them in the future.

Oct. 16 . . . A calm, blue, hazy October day. Sunday, but it brings no changes in the dull monotony of our pent up life.

Oct. 18 . . . Night. It is a quiet hour now. Silence, "like a gentle spirit" is brooding over our noisy camp. The round faced moon is now coming boldly up, and her pale, passionless rays are now gilding the tops of many tents. How quiet!

Oct. 22 . . . Very, very cold today. We have no fire, and tonight I can hardly get warm in my blankets—chilled through.

Oct. 23 . . . This is Sunday. Bright sunshine, but cold blue sky.

Oct. 27 . . . About a thousand prisoners were sent from here yesterday and day before. I thought once I was going, beyond all doubt, but could not. I am now living in the Hospital as registering clerk. A very dark, rainy and stormy night. Have been on this Point exactly one year today.

Oct. 29 . . . Been sick all day—headache, and don't feel well anyhow. Mighty dull and stupid.

Nov. 9 . . . Nothing of interest has transpired since the last date, except the departure of some prisoners for the South. Yesterday was the Presidential election, but we haven't received any news yet. I've quit clerking for a Division in camp, and have a clerkship now in the hospital.

Nov. 16 . . . Received a letter yesterday from Julee containing Jap's photograph. I don't know anyone that resembles the picture! The crew of the Privateer "Florida" came in camp last night. Julee said another box will soon come.

Dec. 1 . . . Received the above mentioned box today. Everything was in perfect order.

Dec. 6 . . . Got a money letter today from Julee containing $5. Went out and sat for my picture. I will get a doz. on the 9th.

Dec. 11 . . . Sunday night. Very dark, rainy and chilly. I think fate has now closed the only hope left us.

Dec. 18 . . . Another Sunday. Nothing new ever transpires with us here. The same old thing over and over. The box I received from home is almost played out.

Dec. 24 . . . Christmas Eve!

Dec. 25 . . . Christmas Day! My mess had mince pie and fried chicken for dinner today. I am mighty down in the mouth today. I want to get out of prison so badly.

Dec. 31 . . . The old year is almost gone, and he is going out in a perfect storm of snow and rain. Received a letter today from Ma.

1865

Feb. 17, 1865. After a month and a half I will commence my diary again. On the 10th I left Point Lookout for Dixie Land, and arrived at this place—Richmond City, on the night of the 14th. I expect to get a 40 day furlough in a few days.

Feb. 19 . . . Got my furlough yesterday and started this morning for Staunton. I was told on the train that Aunt Julia still lived at Fisherville, and I stopped there, but found she had left some time ago. *Couldn't* stay all night, and had to start to Staunton on foot—walked about three miles and got permission to stay all night with a Mr. Koiner.

Feb. 20 . . . Walked to Staunton this morning, but found no one that I knew—stood about at the Hotel (American) and paid $40 per day board, and next morning went back up to Waynesboro to see Mr. Samuel Woods and family. (Note: The Woods family were Philippi residents. Mr. Woods was a Confederate officer in charge of army supplies, and was stationed at Staunton. After the battle of Philippi his wife and children refugeed further South, and lived at Waynesboro until the end of the war.) Was cordially received, and enjoyed myself very much, and shall always remember Mr. Woods for his interest and kindness.

Feb. 23 . . . Came to Staunton this morning, and stayed all night in Mr. Woods's office.

Feb. 24 . . . Left this morning on the train for Millboro, and put up at the "Dickerson Hotel". My coming to this place was with the intention of meeting with a Mr. Lightburn and then to slip through home, and return before my furlough expires.

Feb. 27 . . . Mr. Lightburn did not meet me, and after staying 3 days, this morning I started back to Staunton—intending to go down to Bridgewater. Stopping again with Mr. Woods.

Feb. 28 . . . Can't get conveyance to Bridgewater today. The Yanks are coming up the Valley.

March 1 . . . Stayed with Mr. Woods last night.

March 2 . . . All the Quarter Master and commissary stores are now moved over the mountain. Left Waynesboro this morning before the battle began. Stopped at night at a little village called Batesville, and by the way, am riding a horse belonging to Mr. Woods.

March 3 . . . Left this morning for Nelson Court House. Roads awful. Arrived there after night. Rode 30 miles, or more.

March 4 . . . Started this morning for Buckingham Court House. Came within 3 miles of the city, and could not cross a little river which intervened. Stopped with a Mrs. Bonderant.

March 5 . . . Came to Buckingham C.H. this morning and am stopping comfortably with Mr. Strickler and Mr. Morrall. (Note: Isaac Strickler and L. D. Morrall were Philippi residents, who conducted a store in Buckingham for a year or so during the war. There was a family relationship between Mrs. Strickler and the mother of James Hall.)

March 13 . . . Been here during the entire week, but must leave this morning for the *beautiful* army as all furloughs are revoked. Sold Mr. Woods's horse for $1400. Have had a pleasant time while here and regret to leave very much.

March 22, 1865 . . . The Regt. to which I belong is now stationed immediately east of Petersburg, at which place I came to it on the 16th. The lines of the enemy are only three hundred yds. from us now, and a continual firing is kept up by both sides, especially at night. Our duties are very heavy—one third of the men all the time, and the whole has to be up at four every morning. Our quarters are dug in the ground, and are very small and inconvenient—partially bomb-proof. Many of the men have . . . (illegible) . . . only, but are . . .

by the fortification in their front. All of the entire command expects a battle in a few days. If one *does* come off here, it will surpass anything that has yet occurred. Mr. Mathews of Co. K accidentally shot himself today through the hand. His suffering was great, and his hand was ruined.

March 23 . . . This is election day for Senators and House of Delegates. I'm one of the Clerks. Voted only for Mr. Brannon for the Senate. Very little firing along the lines today. Our men are quiet. I presume we will have to erect another line of Chevaux de frise— (Note: sharp sticks for runners of barbed wire) in front of our works. Evening: We had a truce in front of our Brigade this evening for a few minutes. I exchanged papers with a Yankee. Some of them gave our boys coffee, pocket knives, etc. The truce ended and both parties resumed the firing. The Yankee papers speak of our wavering people, and the inevitable overthrow, as if there were not a Southern soldier in existence.

March 24 . . . Drape received a letter today from Mr. Samuel Woods announcing himself as a candidate for State Senate against Mr. Brannon. Of course it was received too late, and we regret it exceedingly.

March 25, 1865 . . . Strange things transpired here today. Our Division attacked the enemy's works at a certain point, and took them without much loss, but the batteries and lines taken had to be abandoned eventually, at which time we lost many men. The Regt. lost over two-thirds of its entire number, killed, wounded and taken prisoner, and a fearful number are among the first. The dead are now being brought to our lines under Flag of Truce. One of my company has already been recognized. Mr. Frank Marshall, Drape Williamson and Lieut. Bosworth are among the missing, and I am actually afraid to hear from them. I fired over fifty rounds during the engagement and my shoulder is very sore from the rebounding of the gun.

March 26 ... Drape and Bosworth are known to be prisoners. Our loss was nearly 150 killed, and the number of prisoners or wounded is not yet reported. Another Truce today. Exchanged papers. Perry Talbott came to the Regt. today. The first time I have seen him since I was captured at Gettysburg July 5, 1863. He will probably be transferred to cavalry in a few days, as he is disabled from infantry service. I feel mighty lonely since Drape's capture, but have not so much duty to do now, as I am appointed *Acting Adjutant* of the Regiment.

March 27 . . . Official duties are tolerably irksome—quite tired tonight,—but it is better than going on duty every other night. No news of any sort today. The Yankees have been firing particularly close during the entire day.

March 30 . . . Last night near eleven o'clock, the Yankees, all of a sudden opened on our works here with great fury—with musketry and artillery, but did not advance. The shelling was truly terrible on both sides. Frequently as many as twenty mortar bombs could be seen in the air at one time, with their brilliant sparkling fuzes. The affair continued the best part of the night. We do not know the object of the enemy in making the attack. This evening— 4 o'clock—the artillery is rolling ominously on our right. Surely, the "great battle" will not be delayed much longer, although the rain, which has been falling nearly all day, may prevent immediate operations. The trenches are awful places in rainy weather. Received a letter yesterday from Miss Bina Morrall, the first I've received since coming South on exchange.

March 31 . . . A reasonably quiet day has almost passed, although there is no telling what any hour may bring forth. The enemy has been shooting remarkably close during the day—in fact, I think they must have crooked guns, for they can shoot straight down behind our works. Last night a bullet struck my fireplace,—came in at the door. The rumors say that heavy fighting has been going on, to our right, but who lost or won, none here can tell.

One thing is evident—our artillery is not removed, for we hear it yet. Bright blue sky and soft, balmy breezes are cheering to us this evening. How beautiful my far off home must appear, clothed in the genial sunlight of hopeful Spring! But here! Surely God never intended that man should thus live. He loves us as no earthly friend can love us, and He also desires that we be happy while we live in this world, and surely this beautiful green world would be a paradise if man would allow it. Why then has the Almighty permitted such evil times to befall us? It must be for some wise purpose—probably to make us better men. Happier times may yet dawn upon us, and we may then be thankful for all that He has done for us.

April 1 . . . A beautiful day is just closing, calm and tranquil. Nothing new has transpired during the day. Only one man was killed in our Regt. He was shot in the head. The Yanks are very spiteful now, in fact we are in continual danger, as they shoot in our quarters, and along the works where we least expect a bullet to come. Heavy fighting has been going on all day on our left, and I presume the activity of the enemy on other parts of the lines causes those on our front to be more annoying. This is a beautiful country—at least it would be, if this war were ended. Petersburg too, is one of the nicest cities I ever saw, and I know in times of peace, it was a gay, gay city. The citizens too, seem as if they are of a caste of mind which is unassailable by ruin and misfortune, for the same light-hearted gayety seems to exist now as that which characterized the "Cockade City" before the war.

April 2 . . . Sunday morning. Last night was nothing but one eternal fight. The Yanks attacked about 11 o'clock, and kept on with the infernal thing all night. They broke through our lines on the left of the Brigade, but were promptly driven away. J. J. Stuart from Barbour County, belonging to Co. K, was fatally wounded—at least the ball struck him in the head, and his brains are oozing through the aperture. Poor fellow, he had his retiring papers, and would have left the Regiment in a few days.—Evening: 3 o'clock—last night's entertainment slacked this morning, but has continued the whole day. We occasionally move to the right or left along the works to strengthen an exposed point. The fight on our right is raging with fury equal to that on our left last night. Petersburg is catching it today. Several long, spiral clouds of smoke are hanging over the city—showing a number of burning houses. The Yanks are now shelling it across our works. All of us expect to be up tonight again. We frequently have not had a chance to eat for nearly a day at a time. I wonder sometimes how long such active operations will continue, surely it is not very common in this remarkable war.

April 3 . . . The enemy broke our lines to the right of us late yesterday evening, driving our men to the suburbs of the city. Our situation was critical in the extreme, as our only place of crossing the river was in the edge of the city, and close to the enemy, and if he had pushed down a little farther, the entire Division would have been captured. We left our works after dark, and proceeded noiselessly across the river. The lurid glare of the burning city lighted our steps, and cast its spectral shadows on the dark waters beneath. Fine mansions and stately edifices were wrapped in flames, and no doubt a vast portion of the city will be destroyed. We marched all night in the direction of Lynchburg and stopped about noon where we are now —a weary, weary march. Cannon booming in our immediate front.

April 4 . . . Tuesday. We are now encamped on Danville R.R. We resumed our march yesterday at noon and continued it all night to this place. Now 3 o'clock P.M. The Yankees are on our immediate front about 1 1/2 miles distant. "Old Bob" has been along beside us all day. The army seems very much dispirited on account of our evacuating Richmond and Petersburg.

April 5 . . . In line of battle on the Danville R.R. 36 miles from Richmond. Our Division is the rear guard of the army, and our Brigade the rear guard of the Division. Today we abandoned several thousand rounds of artillery ammunition with the caissons. It was spread all over the ground and covered nearly half an acre. While the caissons were being burned the whole mass accidentally took fire, and a terrific explosion occurred. Thousands of shells exploded at once, and filled the air with their fragments. Many men were wounded, and a few killed.

April 6 . . . Marched all night. Wearied nearly to death. The enemy attacked our lines at various places, and could frequently be seen watching our movements. A few minutes ago they attacked our Division, and we all thought a royal fight was coming, but a few rounds from a Battalion of artillery drove them away—at least for the present.—Night—The Yanks returned to the attack and drove our artillery from its position. The command immediately fell back and suffered considerably. Abandoned several wagons today on account of the mud.

April 7 . . . Camped last night on the northern side of the Appomattox river, over which we crossed on the High Bridge. The bridge is a grand structure, averaging 150′ high and nearly a mile long. On resuming the march this morning, the bridge was burned on the enemy's making his appearance. We followed the Railroad (South Side) westward. Our design seems to be to reach Lynchburg. On reaching Farmville the enemy came upon us in tremendous force. Our artillery was quickly moved into position, and the infantry was seen stretching across the rolling fields. All at once the artillery opened on the advancing enemy, and the earth trembled with awful concussion. He was driven back, but only to come again at another point. This time he charged upon one of our batteries, and captured two pieces. Our Division being nearest, was hastily put forward to the rescue. When we came in sight, our artillery was galloping to the rear, with the Yankee infantry yelling at its heels—not fifty steps in the rear. A sharp engagement ensued, the enemy was driven back, and the two captured guns recovered. The enemy exhibits an unusual bravery, so likewise do our own men, but it is rather the energy of despair, for everyone knows and feels that we are fighting against hope itself—when everything is even now lost forever. Our rations have failed and the soldiers live on raw corn and whatever the commissary can gather up in this war worn country.

April 9, 1865—The die is cast. The deed is done. General Lee's army has surrendered to the U.S. forces under General Grant. How strange! The Grand old Army of Northern Virginia—the heroes of a hundred victories, and of world wide fame, surrendering to the enemy! But the Grand old Army is not here. It is dead! From its sixty or seventy thousand it is dwindled down to fifteen thousand! It is all over now! We are now allowed to go home on parole—transportation being furnished us. Our Corps Commander made us a short address this evening, giving us goodbye, etc. and extolling the virtues of General Lee's heroic army. He regretted not having come in the army, saying he could look to heaven and feel justified in all that he had done. He made an affecting speech.

April 10 . . . In camp where we were yesterday. Rolls of all the men are being made out. We expect to leave before long. Gen. Grant surely spared our army any mortification he could prevent. No salutes were fired near us, although we could hear their faint echo far to the rear.

April 11 . . . Today Gen. Lee's order relative to the surrender was presented to us. I will give it in full:

HD Qrs. A.N.Va.
10 April 1865

Gen. Orders No. 9
After four years of arduous service, marked by unsurpassed courage and fortitude, the Army of Northern Virginia has been compelled to

yield to overwhelming numbers and resources. I need not tell you—the heroes of so many hard fought battles—who have remained steadfast to the last, that I have consented to this result from no distrust of you, but feeling that valor and devotion could accomplish nothing, nor could compensate for the loss that would attend the continuance of the contest. I determined to avoid the useless sacrifice of those whose past services have endeared them to their countrymen.

By the terms of this agreement, officers and men can return to their homes and remain there undisturbed until exchanged. You will take with you the satisfaction that proceeds from the consciousness of duty faithfully performed, and I earnestly pray that a merciful God will extend his blessings and protection. With an unceasing admiration of your constancy and devotion to your country, and grateful remembrance of your kind and generous consideration of myself, I bid you an affectionate farewell.

      (Signed) R.E. Lee
        General

April 12 . . . 1865 . . . We marched out within the Yankee lines this morning and "stacked our arms." Saw several acquaintances in the Yankee army. Some of my neighbors. Continued our march to Lynchburg. The Yanks issued us rations without any limit.

April 13 . . . Started on our march and followed the canal toward Lexington. Passed a packet boat after walking a few miles. Camped about 15 miles from Lynchburg.

April 14 . . . Arrived at Lexington after dark. Drew rations and quarters in the outbuildings of the Virginia Military Institute. The Institute itself was burned by the Yankee raiders.

April 15 . . . Today we separated. The majority of us will never meet again. All of us who live in N.W. Virginia have agreed to meet at Hightown on next Saturday, and go through the mountains with Maj. Cooper at our head. Eight of us started at noon and traveled about nine miles.

April 16 . . . Continued our march, stopping at night with a Mr. Morrison, a distance of 32 miles. Very tired tonight.

April 17 . . . Traveled only 8 miles today and stopped with a fellow soldier of the same Regt. by the name of Stewart.

April 18 . . . Slept in a *bed* last night. The first for many months. Will stay all day with Mr. Stewart. Having a pleasant time here. Lots of good things to eat, and resting from my weary marches.

April 19 . . . Started this morning and walked to a brother soldier's—a Mr. Jones, a member of my company. We, (Mr. West and myself) will remain with him tonight.

April 20 . . . Walked only 3 miles today. Stopped at a Mr. Seybert's, whose son was a member of my company, and was killed last October. They treated us very kindly indeed, and we were surely thankful for it, as we were quite tired.

April 21 . . . Traveled over to a Mr. Gunus at Hightown. We are going to start home in the morning. Feeling quite feeble tonight.

April 22 . . . The entire crowd got together about 8 o'clock this morning, when we started over the mountains. Camped at night on top of Cheat mountain at Mr. White's—a distance of 31 miles.

April 23 . . . Very cold this morning. Plenty of ice and snow. Came to Beverly where we had to turn over nearly all of our horses to the Provost Marshal. Camped about 4 miles from the town.

April 24 . . . Came to Philippi and stopped with Aunt Betsy Jarvis.

April 25 . . . Capt. Radabaugh and I walked down on Elk today. Powerfully glad to see the folks at home. It seems a little odd that I am here after being absent so long.

April 27 . . . The Captain left for home today. Sorry to see him leave.

April 28 . . . Went fishing.

AFTERWORD

When James E. Hall returned to his home in the spring of 1865, the fact that during the last year of the war he had risen in rank to that of Regimental Adjutant meant little to him. War weary and depleted in health, his only thought was to resume the peaceful occupation of farming, and to lose himself in the quiet of its normalcy.

Four years later, in 1869, he married Elizabeth, daughter of Lewis and Anna Keyes Wilson, pioneer residents of the area, where the Wilsons were noted mill builders—Lewis Wilson's father having built the first mill on the later site of Philippi.

After his marriage, James Hall acquired his own farm in the Elk Creek locality, and resided there until 1878, when he moved to Philippi. He then became an active promoter of the Grafton and Belington Railroad, and was its manager for five years. He held similar positions with other roads, and engaged in various successful business enterprises.

Lillian, the only child of James E. and Elizabeth Hall, was born Oct. 6, 1870. She became the wife of Charles F. Teter of Barbour County, and they were the parents of two sons, Dwight and Charles, and of a daughter, Elizabeth. Today Elizabeth and her husband Cecil O. Phillips own and occupy the Philippi home of her soldier-grandfather, James E. Hall, and with the birth of their two daughters, Sylvia and Elizabeth, the family continuity with his loved "blue hills of home" was assured.

The house is large and square, with wide halls and high ceilings, and around it grow holly trees that were planted when the house was young. It is located in the northern end of town, not far from the river, where once stood the Wilson mill, and is near the historic covered bridge. It is in this house that the war Diary has remained through the years, and where Sylvia, while still a young girl, first began the arduous task of attempting to decipher its yellowed pages, which she later transcribed.

Her mother, Elizabeth Teter Phillips, as custodian of the Diary, recognizing the importance of its preservation, has determined to have it printed. And thus, in the Centennial year of the Civil War, this contribution to its history is made available to the public.

1961   R.W.D.

www.ingramcontent.com/pod-product-compliance
Lightning Source LLC
Chambersburg PA
CBHW030333100526
44592CB00010B/681